THE
ULTIMATE
JOB SEARCH
LETTERS
BOOK

By the same author...

THE ULTIMATE JOB SEARCH LETTERS BOOK

write the perfect letter and get that job

MARTIN YATE

KOGAN
PAGE

First published in the United States in 1992 as *Cover Letters that Knock 'em Dead* by Adams Media Corporation

First published in Great Britain in 2003 as *The Ultimate Job Search Letters Book* by Kogan Page Limited

Published by arrangement with Adams Media Corporation, 57 Littlefield Street, Avon, MA 02322, USA

Kogan Page Limited
120 Pentonville Road
London N1 9JN
United Kingdom
www.kogan-page.co.uk

British Library Cataloguing in Publication Data

A CIP record for this book is available from the British Library

ISBN 0 7494 4069 4

Typeset by Jean Cussons Typesetting, Diss, Norfolk
Printed and bound in Great Britain by Bell & Bain Ltd, Glasgow

Table of Contents

Read this First

> **There's a cruel paradox at work when it comes to writing job search letters.**

We strive to excel in our professions, expending our energies to become top-notch accountants, lorry drivers, brain surgeons … and we spend little or no time learning to promote ourselves on the printed page. When suddenly our livelihood depends on our ability to compose a compelling written summary of the advantages of working with us, we find ourselves in dire straits.

If we ever developed the necessary skills in school, we find they have long since rusted. Writing it all down for review by others in a position to employ us has simply never made it onto the daily to-do list. Many professionals create the thoughts behind their business communications, but use others to craft (and not always well) the messages themselves.

If you find yourself in this situation at the most inopportune time imaginable – during your job search – take heart. This book will solve your problem quickly. Use it exactly as I recommend in the pages that follow. If you do, you will reap a number of benefits, the most important of which is this:

- Your job hunt and ensuing career will benefit tremendously, because your letters will look great, pack a punch, get read and position you as a mover and shaker worth interviewing.

There are other advantages:

- You won't waste a moment of precious time.
- You'll have the satisfaction of having made a tough, intricate, and vitally important professional challenge a little easier and more enjoyable than it is for most people in your shoes (your competitors, for example).
- You might even have some fun.

Employers go through four distinct stages in reaching a decision on employing someone:

1. Longlist development. Advertising and other sources develop the biggest possible field of qualified candidates.

2. Shortlist development. The long list is screened to rule out also-rans. Those who make the cut are invited in for an interview.

3. Shortlist prioritization. Through a series of two or three interviews, candidates are weeded out. Those still standing are ranked according to various criteria.

4. Shortlist review. After the dust settles, each candidate's strengths and weaknesses are reviewed for one last time before the final decision. The information in the dossier created for every shortlisted candidate plays a key role here. This dossier will contain all the knowledge the company has about you. This will include your CV, job search letter, and any follow-up letters you have been smart enough to send during the interview process.

In each of these steps, letters have a role to play in taking you to the next level. For example, a CV without a covering letter rarely gets any further than the waste-paper basket. A 'To whom it may concern' letter fares little better. A letter with a salutation by names gets read and kept, as will follow-up letters on meetings that make comments on the discussions and issues addressed.

It's estimated that the average piece of business correspondence gets less than 30 seconds of the reader's attention. Even a truly great job search letter will not get much more. In crafting your job search letter, you are not aiming to win a place next to a favourite novel on the reader's bedside table. A powerful letter will win that momentary flash of genuine interest and get your CV read with serious attention. Once that's accomplished, you can use the models for the follow-up letters in this book to help you step up on the four-tiered ladder to the job offer.

Letters help you move through each phase of the cycle and on to the offer in ways most people have never understood. In the fourth step (the shortlist review) the interviewer recalls what happened in each phase of the interview cycle. All notes and documentation in the applicant dossier are reviewed for each candidate. This means that as you pass through each step of the cycle, you are presented with a heaven-sent opportunity to advance your candidacy when the moment of truth finally arrives. You can forward all manner of pertinent information that will identify you as the unquestioned prime choice when that last, most critical evaluation is taking place.

I took a common-sense approach to putting this book together: I collected over 4,000 successful job-search letters from the most cynical professionals in the country, corporate human resources people and professional head-hunters. I approached over a thousand of these people and asked them to provide the truly impressive letters they came across – the letters that made a difference, grabbed attention, and advanced someone's candidacy against tough competition. The cream of the crop can be found within these covers.

From these letters, and from my discussions with professionals in the field, I learnt about certain things that work and don't work when putting together a job search letter. These are explored in detail later on in the book, but there is one overriding factor that virtually all the successful letters shared. It's worth exploring here.

All but a handful of the letters were only one page long. Yours probably should be too. Why is brevity so important? My sources feel that:

1. They don't have time to wade through dense patches of text, and they view those who can't get to the point in a dim light.

2. Second pages get detached and often lack sufficient contact information. (For that matter, first pages often fall short in the same category.)

Perhaps the most overlooked benefit of a comprehensive mail dimension to your job-hunting campaign is that the letters can be working for you while you are investing your time and energy elsewhere. A strong mail dimension to your plan can double or triple your effectiveness. Throughout the book whenever you read the word 'mail' it has a double meaning – regular mail and e-mail. The most effective job-hunting campaign will always use the two media in tandem.

If you use the letters simply as noncustomized templates, you may open a few doors. But the 'real' you will be so different from the letters that the interviewers will eventually be left with a nagging doubt that you aren't all you appear to be.

Browse through the letters in the second half of this book. Not all of them will fit your needs at this moment, but take a look anyway. You will see, on every page, proven methods of getting the good word across to potential employers.

This book will also highlight key phrases and wording techniques that caught the eyes of people whose eyes are usually tough to catch. You will discover a 'rhythm' to the words and phrases that have real impact. Then you'll be able to incorporate them into your own original work.

In choosing the examples for this book, I was pleased to see that the ones that rose to the top were all businesslike, with no gimmickry or cuteness. Some may even seem a little dry to you, but remember: they worked. This collection of successful job-search letters includes the best of the best as determined by corporate gatekeepers and captains of industry who know a winner when they see one. It is just such people who will be evaluating your efforts, and the drawbridge of opportunity will be raised (or lowered) for you depending on their evaluation.

Now let's learn how to put together some jigsaw puzzles. I suggest that you read this book with a highlighter in hand, so you can flag appropriate sections for later reference. That way you'll have a wealth of good ideas you can use after just one read. Then you'll be ready to create your own unique job-search letters that will 'knock 'em dead'.

1

What Is a Job Search Letter?

Do you ever receive junk mail? We all do. What do you do with the stuff marked 'occupant'?

Junk mail never gets the attention a personal letter does. You bin it – either without reading it, or after a quick glance.

Too many employment queries end up being treated as junk mail – and if a piece of correspondence is treated like junk mail, that's what it is. Your job search letter is the personalized factor in the presentation of an otherwise essentially impersonal document, your CV. A good letter sets the stage for the reader to accept your CV as something special. Only if your job search letter and CV do their job will interviews and employment offers result.

When the envelope is opened, your letter is the first thing seen. It can make an indelible first impression. Of course, I'm not saying that the letter alone will get you the job, or even land you the interview, but the letter will help you on the way by getting that CV read with something like serious attention.

The higher up the professional ladder you climb, the more important job search letters become. For the candidate who must demonstrate written communication skills in the execution of daily duties (and that's just about all of us), these letters become a valuable vehicle for demonstrating critical job skills. Mess up here and the door to opportunity could well slam shut.

Step One

Grab your reader's ATTENTION. Do this by using quality stationery and envelopes. Use the same paper your CV is printed on. This way your letter and CV will match and give an impression of balance and continuity. See Chapter 5, 'The Final Product,' for details.

Step Two

Generate INTEREST with the content. Do this by addressing the letter to someone by name and quickly explaining what you have to offer. The first sentence grabs attention, the rest of the paragraph gives the reader the old one-two punch. The rule is: say it strong, say it straight and don't pussy-foot.

Do some research. Even a little can get your letter off to a fast start. A case in point is:

> '*I came across the enclosed article in* Newsweek *magazine and thought it might interest you. It encouraged me to do a little research on your company. I am now convinced of two things: You are the kind of people I want to be associated with, and I have the kind of qualifications you can use.*'

Check out a company's Web site; you will find lots of eye-opening data, including news and press clippings. You can also use search engines to find interesting info about the company by typing in the company name as a keyword.

Of course, in the real world, we can't all apply for jobs with companies that are featured in the big magazines. Here are some more everyday examples.

> '*I have been following the performance of your fund in the* Financial Times. *The record over the last three years shows strong portfolio management. With my experience working for one of your competitors, I know I could make significant contributions ...*'

> '*Recently I have been researching the local* _____ *industry. My search has been for companies that are respected in the field and that provide ongoing training programmes. The name* _____ *keeps coming up as a top company.*'

> '*With the scarcity of qualified and motivated [your desired job title] that exists today, I feel sure that it would be valuable for us to talk.*'

'Within the next few weeks I will be moving from London to _____ . Having researched the companies in my field in my new home town, I know that you are the people I want to talk to ...'

'The state of the art in _____ changes so rapidly that it is tough for most professionals to keep up. I am the exception. I am eager to bring my experience to bear for your company.'

Step Three

Now turn that INTEREST into DESIRE. First, tie yourself to a specific job category or work area. Use phrases like:

'I am writing because ...' or 'My reason for contacting you ...'

'... should this be the case, you may be interested to know ...'

'If you are seeking a _____ , you will be interested to know ...'

'I would like to talk to you about your personnel needs and how I am able to contribute to your department's goals.'

'If you have an opening for someone in this area, you will see that my CV demonstrates a person of unusual dedication, efficiency and drive.'

Next, call attention to your merits with a short paragraph that highlights one or two of your special contributions or achievements:

'I have an economics degree from London and a quantitative analysis approach to market fluctuations. This combination has enabled me consistently to pick the new technology flotations that are the backbone of the growth-oriented mutual fund.'

Similar statements applicable to your area of expertise will give your letter more personal punch. Include any qualifications, contributions and attributes that prove you are someone with plenty of talent to offer. If an advertisement (or a conversation with a potential employer) reveals an aspect of a particular job opening that is not addressed in your CV, it should be included in your job search letter:

'I notice from your advertisement that audio- and video-training experience would be a plus. In addition to the qualifications stated in my enclosed CV, I

*have over five years of experience writing and producing sales and manage-
ment training materials in both these media.'*

Whether you decide to use bullets or list your achievements in short staccato
sentences will be determined in part by the amount of space available on the
page.

Step Four

Here's where your letter turns that DESIRE into ACTION. The action you're
aiming for is that the reader will move straight on to your CV, then call you
in for an interview. You achieve this action with brevity – leave the reader
wanting more.

Make it clear to the reader that you want to talk. Explain when, where, and
how you can be contacted. You can now be *proactive* by telling the reader that
you intend to follow up at a certain time if contact has not been established
by then. The reader may then want to initiate action.

Just as you worked to get the opening right, labour over the closing. It is
the reader's last impression of you; make it strong, make it tight and make it
obvious that you are serious about entering into meaningful conversation.

Useful phrases include:

*'It would be a pleasure to give you more information about my qualifications
and experience ...'*

'I look forward to discussing our mutual interests further ...'

*'While I prefer not to use my employer's time taking personal calls at work,
with discretion I can be reached on _____ .'*

*'I will be in your area around the 20th, and will ring you prior to that date.
I would like to arrange ...'*

*'I hope to speak with you further and will ring the week of _____ to
follow up.'*

*'The chance to meet you would be a privilege and a pleasure, so to this end I
shall ring you on _____.'*

*'I look forward to speaking with you further and will ring in the next few
days to see when our schedules will permit a face-to-face meeting.'*

'May I suggest a personal meeting where you can have the opportunity to examine the person behind the CV.'

'My credentials and achievements are a matter of record that I hope you will examine in depth when we meet ...'

'I look forward to examining any of the ways you feel my background and skills would benefit [name of organization]. I look forward to hearing from you.'

'CVs help you sort out the probables from the possibles, but they are no way to judge the calibre of an individual. I would like to meet you and demonstrate that I have the personality that makes for a successful _____.'

'I expect to be in your area on Tuesday and Wednesday of next week and wonder which day would be best for you. I will ring to determine.' (Because many employed people are concerned about their CV going astray, you may wish to add: 'In the meantime, I would appreciate your treating my application as confidential, since I am currently employed.')

'With my training and hands-on experience, I know I can contribute to _____, and want to talk to you about it in person. When may we meet?'

'After reading my CV, you will know something about my background. Yet, you will still need to determine whether I am the one to help you with current problems and challenges. I would like an interview to discuss my ability to contribute.'

'You can reach me at _____ to arrange an interview. I know that your time investment in meeting me will be repaid amply.'

'Thank you for your time and consideration; I hope to hear from you shortly.'

'May I ring you for an interview in the next few days?'

'A brief phone call will establish whether or not we have mutual interests. Recognizing the demands of your schedule, I will make that call within the week.'

As we have noted, some people feel it is powerful in the closing to state a date – 'I'll ring you on Friday if we don't speak before.' – 'or a date and time'

– 'I'll ring you on Friday morning at 10 am if we don't speak before.' The logic is that you demonstrate that your intent is serious, that you are organized, and that you plan your time effectively (all desirable behavioural traits).

On the other hand, at least one 'authority' has said that the reader would be offended by being 'forced' to sit and await your call. Frankly, in 20 years of being involved in the employing process, I have never felt constrained by such statements; I guess I'm just not the sensitive type. What I look for is the person who doesn't follow through on commitments as promised. Therefore, if you use this approach, keep your promises.

2

The Four Types of Job Search Lettters

There are four types of job search letters. The examples that follow will show you which fits your situation.

The General Job Search Letter

Here is an example of a general job search letter. It has been created using the sample phrases listed earlier in this book (note the <u>underlined text</u>). You, too, can write a dynamite job search letter by using these phrases. Then all you have to do is make the minor adjustments necessary to personalize each document. (This letter should be sent as a result of direct research.)

James Swift
18 Park Street ● London X1 0BB
020 8123 4567

2 October, 20–

Jackson Bethell, Head of Operations
ABC Ltd
Industry Square
London X2 2EF

Dear Jackson Bethell,

Recently I have been researching the leading local companies in data communications. My search has been for companies that are respected in the field and which provide ongoing training programmes. The name of ABC Ltd keeps coming up as a top company.

I am an experienced voice and data communications specialist with a substantial background in IBM environments. If you have an opening for someone in this area, you will see that my CV demonstrates a person of unusual dedication, efficiency and drive. My experience and achievements include:

- The complete redesign of a data communications network, projected to increase efficiency company-wide some 12 per cent.
- The installation and troubleshooting of a Defender II call-back security system for a dial-up network.

I enclose a copy of my CV and look forward to examining any of the ways you feel my background and skills would benefit ABC Ltd. While I prefer not to use my employer's time taking personal calls at work, with discretion I can be reached on 020 8123 4567 to initiate contact. Let's talk!

Yours sincerely,

James Swift

James Swift

Jane Swift
18 Park Street, London X1 0BB
020 8123 4567

David Doors, Director of Marketing   14 January, 20–
ABC Ltd
Industry Square
London X2 2EF

Dear David Doors,

I have always followed the performance of your fund in the *Financial Times.*

Recently your notice regarding a Market Analyst in INVESTORS DAILY caught my eye – and your company name caught my attention – because your record over the last three years shows exceptional portfolio management. Because of my experience with one of your competitors, I know I could make significant contributions.

I would like to talk to you about your personnel needs and how I am able to contribute to your department's goals.

An experienced market analyst, I have an economics background (MSc London) and a strong quantitative analysis approach to market fluctuations. This combination has enabled me to consistently pick the new technology flotations that are the backbone of the growth-oriented mutual fund. For example:

I first recommended ABC Fund six years ago. More recently my clients have strongly invested in XYZ (in the high-risk category), and ABC Growth and Income (for the cautious investor). Those following my advice over the last six years have consistently outperformed the market.

I know that CVs help you sort out the probables from the possibles, but they are no way to judge the personal calibre of an individual. I would like to meet you and demonstrate that along with the credentials, I have the personality that makes for a successful team player.

Yours sincerely,

Jane Swift

Jane Swift

The Executive Briefing

The executive briefing is a different and very effective form of job search letter. You can use it whenever you have some information about an opening from a job ad, an online job posting, or a prior conversation. This kind of letter gets right to the point and makes life easy for the corporate recruiter.

Why send an executive briefing?

1. The initial CV screener might have little understanding of the job or its requirements.

2. Your general CV invariably needs customizing for any specific job. (Overly broad CVs are like 'one-size-fits-all' clothes – one size usually fits none.)

3. Your CV is somewhat (or more than somewhat) out of date and you have to send something out immediately to take advantage of the opportunity of a lifetime.

Based on my extensive experience on both sides of the desk, I developed the executive briefing to increase the odds of your CV getting through to the right people.

How can the executive briefing help you through the screening and multiple interview cycle? To answer this we must begin by acknowledging a painful fact. Your CV, by definition, has drawbacks. It is usually too general to relate your qualifications to each specific job. More than one person will probably be interviewing you, and when this happens, the problems begin.

A manager says 'Spend a few minutes with this candidate and tell me what you think.' Your general CV may be impressive, but the manager rarely adequately outlines the job being filled or the specific qualifications he or she is looking for. This means that other interviewers do not have any way to qualify you fairly and specifically. While the manager will be looking for specific skills relating to projects at hand, the personnel department will be trying to match your skills to the vagaries of the job-description manual.

The executive briefing, which supplements the CV, solves the problem with its layout. It looks like the following:

James Swift
18 Park Street ● London X1 0BB
020 8123 4567

2 October, 20–

Dear Sir/Madam,

While my CV will provide you with a general outline of my work history, my problem-solving abilities and some achievements, I have taken the time to list your current specific requirements and my applicable skills in those areas.

Your Requirements	**My Skills**
1. Management of public reference, etc.	1. Experience as head reference librarian at University of London.
2. Supervision of 14 full-time support employees.	2. Supervised support staff of 17.
3. Ability to work with larger supervisory team in planning, budgeting and policy formation.	3. During my last year I was responsible for budget and reforming circulation rules.
4. CILIP-accredited qualification.	4. CILIP-accredited MA – Information and Library Management.
5. 3 years' experience.	5. 1 year with public library; 2 with University of London.

You will see that my attached CV provides further in-depth background. I hope this will enable you to use your time effectively today.

Yours sincerely,

James Swift

James Swift

The other interviewers will flounder because no one told them what to look for. A chain of events like this, naturally, could reduce your chances of landing a job offer.

An executive briefing sent with a CV provides a comprehensive picture of a thorough professional, plus a personalized, fast and easy-to-read synopsis that details exactly how you can help with an employer's current batch of problems.

The executive briefing assures that each CV you send out addresses the job's specific needs and that every interviewer at that company will be interviewing you for the same job.

The use of an executive briefing is naturally restricted to jobs you have discovered through your own efforts or seen advertised. It is obviously not appropriate when the requirements of a specific job are unavailable.

The Broadcast Letter

The broadcast letter is a simple but effective variation on the job search letter. Much of the information will be culled from your CV, because the intent of the broadcast letter is to *replace* the CV. You would be well advised here to conduct an in-depth analysis of your background in much the same way you would for a CV (see Chapter 4). A broadcast letter can often get you into a telephone conversation with a potential employer, but that employer is usually likely to request a proper CV before seeing you anyway.

You should also know that broadcast letters are most frequently used by mature, successfully established professionals.

Beware: if you don't *have* a CV, you might well have to fill in one of those dreadful application forms. This requires putting your background in the format the employer wants – not the package of your choice. Consequently, I do not advise using this kind of letter as the spearhead or sole thrust of your campaign. Rather, you should use it as an integral part of the campaign in one of these ways:

- For small, highly targeted mailings to specific high-interest companies, where it works as an effective customizing technique.

- For small, highly targeted mailings to specific high-interest jobs about which you have enough detailed knowledge that such a letter would supersede the effectiveness of your CV.

- As an initial thrust, but with the more traditional job search letter and CV already in place for a back-up second mailing. In practice, the cold-mailed broadcast letter often results in a request for a CV, and other times results in a telephone interview and subsequent invitation to a face-to-face interview – with the request that you bring a CV.

- As part of a multiple-contact approach where you are approaching a number of people within a company with personalized letters (see Chapter 6).

- As a back-up approach when your job search letter and CV don't generate the response you want from individual target companies.

- To headhunters. Broadcast letters rarely get passed on to employers without your permission.

Here is what a typical broadcast letter might look like:

Jane Swift
18 Park Street, London X1 0BB
020 8123 4567

2 October, 20–

Dear Employer,

For the past seven years I have pursued an increasingly successful career in the sales profession. Among my accomplishments I include:

SALES
As a regional representative, I contributed £1,500,000, or 16 per cent, of my company's annual sales.

MARKETING
My marketing skills (based on a BSc in marketing) enabled me to increase sales 25 per cent in my economically stressed territory, at a time when colleagues were striving to maintain flat sales. Repeat business reached an all-time high.

PROJECT MANAGEMENT
Following the above successes, my regional model was adopted by the company. I trained and provided project supervision to the entire sales force. The following year, company sales showed a sales increase 12 per cent above projections.

The above was based on my firmly held zero price discounting philosophy. It is difficult to summarize my work in a letter. The only way I can imagine providing you with the opportunity to examine my credentials is for us to talk to each other. I look forward to hearing from you.

Yours faithfully,

Jane Swift

Jane Swift

Recruitment Agencies and Executive Recruiters

You might as well know something about headhunters right from the onset. The best way to get the attention of headhunters is to give them the respect they deserve. They are, after all, the most sophisticated salespeople in the world – they and they alone sell products that talk back!

A headhunter will be only faintly amused by your exhortations 'to accept the challenge' or 'test your skills by finding me a job' in the moments before he or she practises their aim with the remains of your letter and the waste-paper basket. They don't have the time or inclination to indulge such whimsical ideas. So with headhunters – whether they are working for an employment agency or a retained search firm – bear in mind these two rules and you won't go far wrong:

1. Get to the point.

2. Tell the truth. Answer questions truthfully and you will likely receive help. Get caught in a lie and you will have established a career-long distrust with someone who possesses a very diverse and influential list of contacts.

    'I am forwarding my CV, because I understand you specialize in representing clients in the _____ field.'

    'Please find the enclosed CV. As a specialist in the _____ field, I felt you might be interested in the skills of a _____.'

    'Among your many clients there may be one or two who are seeking a person for a position as a _____.'

Remember that in a job search letter sent to executive search firms and employment agencies, you should mention your salary and, if appropriate, your willingness to relocate.

Here is an example of a job search letter you might send to a corporate headhunter:

James Swift
18 Park Street London X1 0BB
020 8123 4567

2 December, 20–

Dear Mr O'Flynn,

As you may be aware, the management structure at _____ will be reorganized in the near future. While I am enthusiastic about the future of the agency under its new leadership, I have elected to make this an opportunity for change and professional growth.

My many years of experience lend themselves to a management position in any medium-sized service firm, but I am open to other opportunities. Although I would prefer to remain in London, I would entertain other areas of the country, if the opportunity warrants it. I am currently earning £40,000 a year.

I have enclosed my CV for your review. Should you be conducting a search for someone with my background at the present time or in the near future, I would greatly appreciate your consideration. I would be happy to discuss my background more fully with you on the phone or in a personal interview.

Yours sincerely,

James Swift

James Swift

enclosures

3

What Goes In, What Stays Out

Once upon a time, there were just a few set rules for writing a great job search letter.

The rules of the game have changed; now, more than ever, communication is a prerequisite for any job. Saying 'I'm a great engineer. Give me a chance and I'll prove it to you' just doesn't cut it any more. It is no longer feasible to take employees on approval. Today, job skills and behavioural traits are under close scrutiny throughout the selection process. The process starts the moment you make contact – and that means the content and style of your job search letter had better be up to snuff.

If there is one overriding objective for your job search and follow-up letters, it is to demonstrate your awareness and possession of the learnt behavioural traits that make for successful professionals and good employees.

Developing Personal, Professional, Achievement and Business Profiles

There are 20 universally admired key personality or behavioral traits; they are your passport to success. When reading your letter, the interviewer will search for clues to determine what kind of person you really are and what you would be like to work with.

Personal Profile

Use these words and phrases to project a successful, healthy personal profile.

Drive: A desire to get things done. Goal-oriented.

Motivation: Enthusiasm and a willingness to ask questions. A company realizes a motivated person accepts added challenges and does that little bit extra on every job.

Communication Skills: More than ever, the ability to talk and write effectively to people at all levels in a company is a key to success.

Chemistry: The company representative is looking for someone who does not get rattled, wears a smile, is confident without self-importance, and gets along with others – in short, a team player.

Energy: Someone who always gives that extra effort in the little things as well as more important matters.

Determination: Someone who does not back off when a problem or situation gets tough.

Confidence: With every level of employee – neither intimidated by nor overly familiar with the big cheeses.

Professional Profile

All companies seek employees who respect their profession and employer. Projecting these traits will identify you as loyal, reliable and trustworthy.

Reliability: Following up on yourself, not relying on anyone else to ensure the job is done well, and keeping management informed every step of the way.

Honesty/Integrity: Taking responsibility for your actions, both good and bad. Always making decisions in the best interests of the company, never on a whim or personal preference.

Pride: Pride in a job well done. Always making sure the job is done to the best of your ability. Paying attention to the details.

Dedication: Doing whatever it takes in time and effort to see a project through to completion, on deadline.

Analytical Skills: Weighing the pros and cons. Not jumping to the first possible solution to a problem. Being able to weigh the short- and long-term benefits of a solution against all its possible negatives.

Listening Skills: Listening and understanding, as opposed to jumping in to speak first.

Achievement Profile

Companies have very limited interests: making money, saving money (the same as making money), and saving time, which does both. Projecting your achievement profile, in however humble a fashion, is the key to winning any job.

> *Money Saved:* Every penny saved by your thought and efficiency is a penny earned for the company.
> *Time Saved:* Every moment saved by your thought and efficiency enables your company to save money and make more money in the additional time available. Double bonus.
> *Money Earned:* Generating revenue is the goal of every company.

Business Profile

Projecting your business profile is important on those occasions when you cannot demonstrate ways you have made money, saved money, or saved time for previous employers. These keys demonstrate you are always on the lookout for opportunities to contribute.

> *Efficiency:* Always keeping an eye open for wasted time, effort, resources and money.
> *Economy:* Most problems have two solutions: an expensive one and one that the company would prefer to implement.
> *Procedures:* Procedures exist to keep the company profitable. Don't work around them. This means keeping your boss informed. Tell your boss about problems or good ideas, and don't go over his or her head. Follow the chain of command. Do not implement your own 'improved' procedures or organize others to do so.
> *Profit:* The reason all the above traits are so universally admired in the business world is that they relate to profit.

Your goal is to draw attention to as many of these traits as possible by direct statement, inference, or illustration.

Writing a job search letter is a bit like baking a cake. In most instances the ingredients are essentially the same – what determines the flavour is the order and quantity in which those ingredients are blended. There are certain ingredients that go into almost every letter, whether job search, broadcast, networking, follow-up, acceptance, rejection, or resignation letters. There are others that rarely or never go in, and there are those special touches (a pinch of this, a smidgen of that) that may be included, depending on your personal tastes and the need your letter will satisfy.

Brief Is Beautiful

Ads and job search letters have a great deal in common. The vast majority of ads in any media can be heard, watched, or read in under 30 seconds – the upper limit of the average consumer's attention span.

It is no coincidence that both job search letters and CVs adhere to the same rules that govern all forms of writing. They need to be absorbed in less than 30 seconds. They are business communication, and business likes to get to the point.

Before getting started, good copywriters imagine themselves in the position of their target audience. They know their objective: to sell something. Then they consider what features their product possesses and what benefits it holds for the purchaser. This invariably requires some understanding of the target or targets.

For the next 15 minutes, imagine yourself in one of your target companies. You are in the personnel department on 'screening' detail. Fortunately, it is a slow morning and there are only 30 CVs and job search letters that need to be read. Go straight to the example sections of this book now and read 30 examples without a break, then return to this page. You will probably feel disoriented, as if your brain has turned to mush.

Now you have some idea of what it feels like, except that you had it easy. The letters you read were good, interesting ones – letters that got real people real jobs. Even so, you probably felt a little punch drunk at the end of the exercise. But you learnt a very valuable lesson: brevity is beautiful. Can you imagine what it might be like to do this every day for a living?

The first thing you have to do is understand why some people get the job while others don't. Then look at your own background in a way that will enable you to get your point across. Every decision to employ is made on a job applicant's ability to satisfy these five concerns of the employer:

1. Ability and suitability.
2. Willingness to go the extra yard, to take the rough with the smooth.
3. Manageability: taking direction and constructive input in a positive and professional manner.
4. Problem-solving attitude.
5. Supportive behavioural traits.

A Question of Money

Ads often request salary information. With the right letter you will rarely be denied at least a telephone conversation, even if you do omit your salary history. Nevertheless, there may be factors that make you feel obliged to include something. I have heard that some personnel people consider the word 'negotiable' annoying, though perhaps not grounds for refusing to see an applicant.

If you choose to share information about salary, it must go on the job search letter or be attached to it. It should never go on the CV itself. If you choose not to include it, the contact can always ask you. When you're asked to state the salary you're looking for, don't restrict yourself to one figure; instead, give yourself a range with a spread between the low and the high end. This dramatically increases your chances of 'clicking onto' the available salary range.

When salary history is requested, the prospective employer is usually looking for a consistent career progression. Gaps or significant cuts could raise red flags. If you have nothing to hide and have a steadily progressive earnings history, spell it out on a separate sheet.

Many of us have less than perfect salary histories for any number of perfectly valid reasons. Consequently, we don't want to release these figures unless we are there in person to explain away the seeming anomalies. In these instances the matter is best skirted in the job search letter itself.

Here is one way to address the topic of money in your letters should you feel it is appropriate to do so. You will find others later in the book.

> *'My salary requirements are in the £ _____ to £ _____ range, with appropriate benefits. I would be willing to relocate for the right opportunity.'*

Telephone and E-mail

Once you have determined a primary contact number you must ensure that it will be answered at all times. There is no point in mounting a job-hunting campaign if prospective and eager employers can never reach you. Invest in an answering machine or hire an answering service. If your choice is an answering machine, keep the message businesslike. Once recorded, call the machine from another phone. Are you impressed?

You also need an alternative number; if at all possible, it should be answered by someone who is just about always there (perhaps a family member). Always list your e-mail address immediately beneath your telephone number.

Ingredients: A Basic Checklist

Skip ahead to the sample letters in Chapter 8. As you read through a few of them, bear in mind that for your letters to be effective, they must:

- Address a person, not a title ... and whenever possible, a person who is in a position to make the decision on whether to employ you.

- Be tailored to the reader as far as is practical, to show that you have done your homework.

- Show concern, interest and pride for your profession.

- Demonstrate energy and enthusiasm.

- Get to the point.

- Avoid stuffiness, and maintain a balance between professionalism and friendliness.

- Include information relevant to the job you are seeking.

- Ask for the next step in the process clearly and without apology or arrogance.

Finally, notice the variety of letters there are – you have many examples to help you maximize both the volume and the value of your offers.

4

Assembling Your Job Search Letter

> There is a fine line between pride in achievement and insufferable arrogance when listing experiences and behaviours in your work life that will help advance your candidacy.

To create the building blocks of your job search letter, complete the questionnaire on the next couple of pages. Do not skip this exercise; the self-knowledge you develop will be of real help when the time comes to sell yourself at the interview. Answer the questions for every job you have held, starting with the most recent and working backwards.

Take some time over this exercise and go back carefully over past jobs. Your answers to this questionnaire will form the meat of your letters. It isn't going to be necessary to craft 'knock 'em dead' sentences from scratch, although (believe it or not) you could, given the time and commitment. With the help of this book you'll be able to cut and paste with the best of them – your end result being a unique and arresting letter.

However, the entirely original parts of your constructed letter will be those areas that address your contributions and achievements. That means you need to spend adequate time on this period of preparation. What you jot down here will later be crafted into punchy sentences.

About the Questionnaire

This questionnaire was taken from the comprehensive 'Skills Analysis' questionnaire in *Resumes That Knock 'em Dead*. Completion of this comprehensive evaluation tool will reward the prudent professional.

Questionnaire

FOR EACH OF YOUR PREVIOUS JOBS:
List three to five major duties:

_____

_____

_____

FOR EACH OF THESE DUTIES:
What special skills or knowledge did you need to perform these tasks satisfactorily?

_____

_____

_____

What was the biggest problem you faced in this area?

_____

_____

_____

What was your solution, and the result of the solution?

_____

_____

_____

What was your biggest achievement in this area? Think about money made (or saved) or time saved for the employer.

_____

_____

_____

What verbal or written comments did your peers or managers make about your contributions in this area?

_____

_____

_____

What was the greatest contribution in this area you made as a team player?

_____

_____

_____

What desirable behavioural traits did you demonstrate in this area to get the job done?

_____

_____

_____

Now that you've completed the questionnaire, it's time to put your responses to work for you.

Creating Punchy Sentences

Concise, punchy sentences grab attention.

The most grammatically correct sentences in the world won't get you interviews (except perhaps as a copy editor – and then not always) because such prose can read as though every breath of life has been squeezed out of it.

Sentences gain power with verbs that demonstrate an action. For example, one professional – with a number of years at the same law firm in a clerical position – had written:

'_I learnt to manage a computerized database._'

Pretty ordinary, right? Well, after discussion of the circumstances that surrounded learning how to manage the computerized database, certain exciting facts emerged. By using action verbs and an awareness of employer interests, this sentence was charged up and given more punch. Not only that, but for the first time the writer fully understood that value of her contributions, which greatly enhanced her self-image:

> *'I <u>analysed</u> and <u>determined</u> the need for automation of an established law office. I was <u>responsible</u> for hardware and software selection, installation and loading. Within one year, I had <u>achieved</u> a fully automated office. This <u>saved</u> 40 hours a week.'*

Notice how the verbs show that things happened when she was around the office. These action verbs and phrases add an air of direction, efficiency and accomplishment to every letter. Succinctly, they tell the reader what you did and how well you did it.

Rewrite each of your query answers using action verbs to give them punch. To help you in the process, here are over 175 action verbs you can use. This list is just a beginning. Every word processing program has a thesaurus; type in any one of these words and get 10 more for each entry.

Varying Sentence Structure

Good writers are at their best when they write short punchy sentences. Keep your sentences under about 20 words; a good average is around 15. If your sentence is longer than the 20 mark, change it. Either shorten it by restructuring or make two sentences out of one. However, you will want to avoid choppiness. Try to vary the length of sentences when you can.

You can also start with a short phrase ending in a colon:

- followed by bullets of information;
- each one supporting the original phrase.

All of these techniques are designed to enliven the reading process. An example follows.

accomplished
achieved
acted
adapted
addressed
administered
advanced
advised
allocated
analysed
appraised
approved
arranged
assembled
assigned
assisted
attained
audited
authored
automated
balanced
budgeted
built
calculated
catalogued
chaired
clarified
classified
coached
collected
compiled
completed
composed
computed
conceptualized
conducted
consolidated
contained
contracted
contributed
controlled
coordinated
corresponded
counselled
created

critiqued
cut
decreased
delegated
demonstrated
designed
developed
devised
diagnosed
directed
dispatched
distinguished
diversified
drafted
edited
educated
eliminated
enabled
encouraged
engineered
enlisted
established
evaluated
examined
executed
expanded
expedited
explained
extracted
fabricated
facilitated
familiarized
fashioned
focused
forecast
formulated
founded
generated
guided
identified
illustrated
implemented
improved
increased
indoctrinated

influenced
informed
initiated
innovated
inspected
installed
instigated
instituted
instructed
integrated
interpreted
interviewed
introduced
invented
launched
lectured
led
maintained
managed
marketed
mediated
moderated
monitored
motivated
negotiated
operated
organized
originated
overhauled
oversaw
performed
persuaded
planned
prepared
presented
prioritized
processed
produced
programmed
projected
promoted
provided
publicized
published
purchased

recommended
reconciled
recorded
recruited
reduced
referred
regulated
rehabilitated
remodelled
repaired
represented
researched
restored
restructured
retrieved
revitalized
saved
scheduled
schooled
screened
set
shaped
solidified
solved
specifiied
stimulated
streamlined
strengthened
summarized
supervised
surveyed
systemized
tabluated
taught
trained
translated
travelled
trimmed
upgraded
validated
worked
wrote

Analysed and determined need for automation of an established law office:

- Responsible for hardware and software selection.

- Coordinated installation of six work stations.

- Operated and maintained equipment; trained other users.

- Full automation achieved in one year.

- Savings to company: £25,000.

KISS (Keep It Simple, Stupid)

Just as you use short sentences, use common action words. They communicate quickly and are easy to understand. Stick to short, simple words whenever possible (without sounding infantile).

Communicating, persuading and motivating your readers to take action is challenging, because many people in different companies will see your letters and make judgements based on them. This means you must keep industry 'jargon' to a minimum (especially in the initial contact letters – job search, broadcast and the like). There will be those who understand the intricacies and technicalities of your profession – but unfortunately, many of the initial screeners do not. You'll need to share your specialist wisdom with the non-specialists first, before you can expect to reach your professional peers.

> *Short words for short sentences help make short, gripping paragraphs: good for short attention spans!*

Within your short paragraphs and short sentences, beware of name dropping and acronyms, such as 'I worked for Dr A Witherspoon in Sys. Gen. SNA 2.31.' Such statements are too restricted to have validity outside the small circle of specialists to whom they speak. Unless you work in a highly technical field, avoid doing this. Your letters demand the widest possible appeal, yet they need to remain personal in tone. (Of course, you don't want your letters to sound like they're from the Reader's Digest, either.)

Voice and Tense

The voice you use for different letters depends on a few important factors:

- Getting a lot said in a small space.

- Being factual.

- Packaging yourself in the best way.

- Using what feels good to you.

The voice you use in your letters should be consistent throughout. There is considerable disagreement among the 'experts' about the best voice, and each of the following options have both champions and detractors.

Sentences in all types of job search letters can be truncated (up to a point), by omitting pronouns and articles such as _I, you, he, she, it, they, a_, or _the_:

> _'Automated office.'_

In fact, many authorities recommend the dropping of pronouns as a technique that both saves space and allows you to brag about yourself without seeming boastful. It gives the impression of another party writing about you. Others feel that to use the personal pronoun – 'I automated the office ...' – is naive, unprofessional, and smacks of boasting.

At the same time, some recommend that you write in the first person because it makes you sound more human.

> _'I automated the office.'_

In short, there are no hard and fast rules – they can all work given the many unique circumstances you will face in any given job hunt. Use whatever style works best for you. If you do use the personal pronoun, try not to use it in every sentence – it gets a little monotonous, and it can make you sound like an egomaniac. The mental focus is not 'I' but 'you,' the person with whom you are communicating.

A nice variation is to use a first-person voice throughout the letter and then a final few words in the third person. Make sure these final words appear in the form of an attributed quote, as an insight to your value:

> _'She managed the automation procedure, and we didn't experience a moment of down time.'_
> _– Jane Ross, Department Manager_

Don't mistake the need for professionalism in your job search letters with stiff-necked formality. The most effective tone is one that mixes the conversational and the formal, just the way we do in our offices and in our jobs. The only overriding rule is to make the letter readable, so that the reader can see a human being shining through the pages.

Length

The standard length for a job search letter is usually one page, or the equivalent length for e-mails. Subsequent letters stemming from verbal communications – whether over the telephone or face to face – should also adhere to the one-page rule, but can run to two pages if complexity of content demands it. Generally speaking, no job search letter should exceed two pages. Break this rule at your peril; to do so will brand you as a windbag incapable of getting to the point.

Having said this, I should acknowledge that all rules are made to be broken. Occasionally a three-page letter might be required, but only in one of the following two instances:

1.   You have been contacted directly by an employer about a specific position and have been asked to present data for that particular opportunity.

2.   An executive recruiter who is representing you determines that the exigencies of a particular situation warrant a dossier of such length. (Often such a letter and CV will be prepared exclusively – or with considerable input – by the recruiter.)

You'll find that thinking too much about length will hamper the writing process. Think instead of the story you have to tell, then layer fact upon fact until your tale is told. Use your words and the key phrases from this book to craft the message of your choice. When *that* is done you can go back and ruthlessly cut it to the bone.

Ask yourself these questions:

- Can I cut out any paragraphs?
- Can I cut out any sentences?
- Can I cut out any superfluous words?
- Where have I repeated myself?

If in doubt, cut it out – leave nothing but facts and action words! If at the end you find too much has been cut, you'll have the additional pleasure of reinstating your deathless prose.

Your Checklist

There are really two proofing steps in the creation of a polished job search letter. The first happens now. You want to make sure that all the things that should be included are – and that all the things that shouldn't, aren't. The final proofing is done before printing. Warning: it is easy, in the heat of the creative moment, to miss crucial components or mistakenly include facts that give the wrong emphasis. Check all your letters against these points:

Contact Information

■ The pertinent personal data (name, address, postcode, personal telephone number and e-mail address) are on every page.

■ Your business number is omitted unless it is absolutely necessary and safe to include it.

■ If your letter is more than one page long, each page is numbered 'page 1 of 2,' etc., and all the pages are stapled together. Remember the accepted way of stapling business communications: one staple in the top left-hand corner. Contact info, at least name, telephone numbers and e-mail address, should be on each page.

Objectives

■ Does your letter state why you are writing?

■ Is the letter tied to the target company and job (if you have details)?

■ Does it address points of relevance, such as skills that apply from the ad or agenda items addressed at the interview?

■ Does it include references to some of your personality or behavioural traits that are crucial to success in your field?

■ Is your most relevant and qualifying experience prioritized to lend strength to your letter?

■ Have you avoided wasting more space than required with employer names and addresses?

■ Have you omitted any reference to reasons for leaving a particular job? Reasons for change might be important at the interview, but they are not relevant at this point. Use this precious space to sell, not to justify.

■ Unless they have been specifically requested, have you removed all references to past, current, or desired salaries?

■ Have you removed references to your date of availability? Remember, if you aren't available at their convenience, why are you wasting their time?

■ If your education is mentioned, is it relevant to the advertisement?

■ Is your highest educational attainment the one you mention?

■ Have you avoided listing irrelevant responsibilities or job titles?

■ Have you mentioned your contributions, your achievements and the problems you have successfully solved during your career?

■ Have you avoided poor focus by eliminating all extraneous information? ('Extraneous' means anything that doesn't relate to your job objective, such as captaining the tiddlywinks team in playschool.)

■ Is the whole thing long enough to whet the reader's appetite for more details, yet short enough not to satisfy that hunger?

■ Have you left out lists of references and only mentioned the availability of references (if, of course, there is nothing more valuable to fill up the space)? To employers this is a given. If you aren't prepared to produce them on demand, you simply won't get the job.

■ Have you let the obvious slip in, like heading your letter 'Letter of Application' in big bold letters? If so, cut it out.

Writing Style

■ Substitute short words for long words, and one word where previously there were two.

■ Keep your average sentence to 10 to 20 words. Shorten any sentence of more than 20 words or break it into two sentences.

■ Keep every paragraph under five lines, with most paragraphs shorter.

■ Make sure your sentences begin with or contain, wherever possible, powerful action verbs and phrases.

■ If you are in a technical field, don't overload with technical jargon, unless you are certain a specific reader will understand your message. This is most important in job search and broadcast letters: they are likely to be screened by non-techies. Part of their job is to assist in the employment of techies who can communicate with the rest of the human race. In subsequent letters to fellow techies, however, the technical jargon may not only be desirable but mandatory to get your point across.

5

The Final Product

Style – so easy to see but so difficult to define – usually has a distinct look and feel. Here are some of the basics you should keep in mind when creating your own stylish and professional job search letters.

Layout

The average job search letter arrives on a desk along with as many as 50 or 60 others, all of which require screening. You can expect your letter to get a maximum of 30 seconds attention, and that's only if it's accessible to the reader's eye.

The biggest complaints about job search letters that nosedive into the waste-paper basket in record time are:

- They have too much information crammed into the space and are therefore hard on the eyes.

- The layout is disorganized, illogical and uneven. (In other words, it looks shoddy and slapdash – and who wants an employee like that?)

- In the age of spellcheckers, there are no excuses for misspellings, and none are accepted.

Fonts

Choose business-like fonts; stay away from script-like fonts or those that have serifs. They may sometimes look more visually exciting, but the goal is to be kind to the tired eyes of the reader who is plowing through stacks of CVs when he or she gets your message. Capitalized copy is also harder to read and causes eye strain.

How to Brighten the Page

Once you decide on a font, stick with it. More than one font on a page can look confusing. You can do plenty to liven up the visual impact of the page within the variations of the font you have chosen. You can, of course, use a different font for the contact information as you create the letterhead.

Most fonts come in a selection of regular, bold, italic and bold italic. Good job search letters will take judicious advantage of this. You can vary the impact of key words with italics, underlined phrases, and boldface or capitalized titles for additional emphasis. There are a lot of options, but these options won't work with e-mail, as the e-mail won't retain your formatting. There is a good lesson here: you can brighten the page, but the words alone must be able to carry your message!

You will notice from the occasional example in this book that some letters use more than one typographical variation of the same font. For example, a writer who wants to emphasize personality traits might italicize only those words or phrases that describe these aspects. That way the message gets a double fixing in the reader's mind. You will also notice powerful letters that employ no typographical pyrotechnics and still 'knock 'em dead'! In the end, it's your judgement call.

If you are crafting letters that are general in content, you will need to use the mail merge feature of the word-processing program. What this does is fill in the blanks: 'Dear _____' becomes 'Dear Fred Jones.'

> *Dear* Fred Jones:
> *Your* 11 January, 2001 *ad in the* Daily Telegraph *described a need for an accountant.*

All this does is state loud and clear that this is a form letter sent, in all likelihood, to hundreds. Why needlessly detract from your chances of being taken seriously?

Another no-no is the use of 'clip art' to brighten the page. Those little quill pens and scrolls may look nifty to you, but they look amateurish to the rest of the business world.

Employing Professionals

Those who wish to use professionals to produce their letters have more than one option to choose from.

Using a Word-Processing Service

Any reader who can use a computer can skip this paragraph; hopefully that is just about everyone. However, if you have just been returned to the earth by aliens, there are a couple of things you should know. Things have changed since you've been gone and now we all have personal computers. If you don't learn to use one quickly, you are 'up the creek without a paddle.' That being said, if you need to use a service for any reason, here's what to watch out for.

Small companies come and go with great rapidity, so when your job search letter is finished, ask for three copies of it on separate disks. Why three? Funny things can happen to disks. (I once lost half a book because of disk malfunction.) Consequently, everyone with a computer should always maintain two back-up copies of the original document, *each on a separate disk*, making a total of three copies. This way, no matter where you find yourself living next time your career demands a job hunt, your letters are ready for updating. By the way, you should not be charged more than a couple of pounds for each back-up disk. Even the best-quality disks are cheap, and the copying process takes maybe 60 seconds to complete. Negotiate the cost of the copies before you assign the project; that way you won't have the unpleasantness of an unscrupulous operator trying to take advantage of you. (Helpful hint: Be sure the label on the disk identifies the software environment in which the letters were composed.)

Proofing

It simply isn't possible for even the most accomplished professional writer to go from draft to print, so don't try it. Your pride of authorship will hide blemishes you can't afford to miss.

You need some distance from your creative efforts to give yourself detachment and objectivity. There is no hard and fast rule about how long it should take to come up with the finished product. Nevertheless, if you think you have finished, leave it alone at least overnight. Then come back to it fresh. You'll read it almost as if you were seeing it for the first time.

Before you print your letters make sure that what you've written is as clear as possible. Three things guaranteed to annoy readers are incorrect spelling, poor grammar and improper syntax. Go back and check all these areas. If you think syntax has something to do with the Inland Revenue, you'd better get a third party involved. An acquaintance of mine came up with an eminently practical solution. She went to the library, waited for a quiet moment, and got into a conversation with the librarian, who subsequently agreed to give her letter the old once-over. (Everyone loves to show off special knowledge!)

The quality of paper always makes an impression on the person holding the page. The people receiving your letter see literally dozens of others every day, and you need every trick available to make your point. The weight of high-quality paper compared to the flimsy copying paper sends an almost subliminal message about certain personality traits, most notably attention to detail. Another reason for using high-quality paper for your letters is that it takes the ink better, therefore giving you clean, sharp print resolution.

By the way, if an emergency demands you send a letter by fax, remember to follow it up with a copy on regular paper. This is because everything you send is likely to end up in your 'candidate dossier.' A fax can obliterate important parts of any communication.

Although you should not skimp on paper costs, neither should you buy or be talked into using the most expensive available. Indeed, in some fields (health care and education come to mind), too ostentatious a paper can give a negative impression. The idea is to create a feeling of understated quality.

As for colour, white is considered the prime choice. Cream is also acceptable, and I'm assured that some of the pale pastel shades can be both attractive and effective. These pastel shades were originally used to make letters and CVs stand out. But now everyone is so busy standing out of the crowd in magenta and passionate puce that you just might find it more original to stand out in white or cream. White and cream are straightforward, nononsense colours. They say BUSINESS.

It is a given that letter stationery should always match the colour and weight of your envelopes and CV. To send a white letter – even if it is your personal stationery – with a cream CV is gauche and detracts from the powerful statement you are trying to make. In fact, when you print the finished letter, you should print some letterhead sheets at the same time and in the same quantity. It should be in the same font and on the same kind of paper. You don't need to get too fancy; base your design on other stationery you've been impressed with.

All subsequent letters should be on the same paper. Your written communication will be filed. Then, prior to the decision on whom to employ, the manager responsible will review all the data on all the short-listed candidates. Your coordinated written campaign will paint the picture of a thorough professional. The sum of your letters will be more powerful as a whole simply because there will be continuity of form and content.

Envelopes Send Messages Too

What goes on the envelope affects the power of the message inside. Over the last six months, I've asked a number of line managers and human resources professionals about the envelope's appearance. Does it affect the likelihood of the letter being read and if so, with what kind of anticipation? Here's what I heard:

'I never open letters with printed pressure-sensitive labels; I regard them as junk mail, and I simply don't have the time in my life for ill-targeted marketing attempts.'

'I never open anything addressed to me by title but not by name.'

'I will open envelopes addressed to me by misspelt name, but I am looking with a jaundiced eye already; and that eye is keen for other examples of sloppiness.'

'I always open correctly typed envelopes that say personal and/or confidential, but if they're not, I feel conned. I don't hire con artists.'

'I always open neatly handwritten envelopes. What's more, I open them first, unless there's another letter that is obviously a cheque.'

There are those who recommend enclosing a stamped self-addressed envelope to increase the chances of response. You can do this, but don't expect many people in the corporate world to take advantage of your munificence. I have never known this tactic to yield much in the way of results. On the whole, I think you are better advised to save the stamp money and spend it on a follow-up telephone call. Only conversations lead to interviews. I have never heard of a single interview being set up exclusively through the mail.

(*Neat trick department*: I recently received an intriguing CV and job search letter; both had attached to the top right-hand corner a circular red sticker. It worked as a major exclamation point; I was impressed. I was even more impressed when I realized that once this left my hands, no other reader would know exactly who attached the sticker, but they *would* pay special attention to the content because of it. Nice technique; don't let the whole world in on it, though.)

Appearance

Remember that the first glance and feel of your letter can make a powerful impression. Go through this checklist before you seal the envelope:

- Is the paper A4-sized and is it of good quality, 100 grams per square metre (gsm) in weight?

- Have you used white, off-white, or cream-coloured paper?

- Did you make sure to use only one side of the page?

- Are your name, address and telephone number on every page?

- If more than one page, have you numbered your letter: '1 of 2' and so on at the bottom of the page?

- Are the pages stapled together? Remember, one staple in the top left-hand corner is the accepted protocol.

6

The Plan of Attack

Great job search, broadcast and follow-up letters won't get you a job by sitting on your desk like rare manuscripts. You have to do something with them.

Even a company with a zero growth rate can still be expected to experience a turnover in staff in the course of a year. In other words, every company has openings *sometimes*, and any one of those openings could have your name on it.

The problem is you won't have the chance to pick the very best opportunity unless you check them all out. Every intelligent job hunter will use a six-tiered approach to cover all the bases:

- Internet job postings
- Newspaper advertisements
- Personal and professional networking
- Direct-researched opportunities
- Recruitment agencies
- Business and trade publications

Online Job Postings

Here is where the Internet can play an especially useful role. There are hundreds of job banks that advertise vacancies called 'job postings' in Internet speak; almost every one of these sites has a CV bank. When you place your CV in a CV bank, it is available for view by any employer or headhunter. So long as there is a privacy feature to protect your identity, this is a very good marketing tool.

Here's how to use them to greatest effect.

Visit the job banks and search for appropriate job openings. Most of these job banks have a powerful device called an 'e-mail alert.' The alert allows you to identify the type of work you are seeking and receive an e-mail from the site every time a suitable job is advertised by one of their clients. You don't want these e-mails to come to you indiscriminately at work, so be sure to use your personal e-mail address.

The CV banks will work well for you too. From an employer's point of view, these CV banks are like big fish tanks. The fishing analogy works for you too: your CV in CV banks is like having a baited hook in the water while you go about your business. CV banks often delete your CV after 90 days, so if you are looking longer than this you will need to go back and reload. Actually, it is not a bad idea to keep a CV posted on an ongoing basis; it will keep you aware of who is looking for what and how much they are paying. It's like keeping your finger on the pulse of the market. Use the free online course at careerbrain.com.

If you are writing as a result of an online job posting, you should mention both the Web site and the date you found it:

> *'I read your job posting on your company's Web site on 5 January and felt I had to respond…'*

> *'Your online job posting regarding a _____ on CareerCity.com caught my eye, and your company name caught my attention.'*

> *'This e-mail, and my attached CV, are in response to your job posting on _____.'*

See more about online job search letters in Chapter 7.

Job Advertisements

A first step for many is to go to the job ads and do a mass mailing. Bear in mind, there should be a method to your madness when you do this. Remember, if it is the first idea that comes to *your* mind, hitting the job ads will be at the front of everyone else's thoughts, too.

A single job advertisement can draw hundreds of responses. The following ideas might be helpful:

- Most newspapers have an employment section every week, when, in addition to their regular advertising, they have a major drive for recruitment ads. Make sure you always read this edition of your paper.

■ So-called authorities on the topic will tell you not to rely on the job ads – that they don't work. Rockinghorse droppings! Job ads don't work only if you are too dumb to know how to use them. Look for back issues. Just because a company is no longer advertising does not necessarily mean that the vacancy has been filled. The employer may well have become disillusioned, and is now using a professional recruiter to work on the position. They may have filled the position; perhaps the person never started work or simply did not work out in the first few months. Maybe they took on someone who did work out and now they want someone else. When you go back into the job ads you'll find untold opportunities awaiting you, and instead of competition from 150 other job hunters responding to this week's job ad there may be just one or two people vying for the slot.

■ I had a letter from a reader recently who told me he had landed a £60,000 job from a seven-month-old job ad he came across in a pile of newspapers in his father-in-law's garage! (You see? There is a use for in-laws, after all.)

■ In many instances jobs are available but just aren't being advertised. It's what the press refers to as the 'hidden job market'. Likewise, in some high-demand occupations where job ads aren't famous for drawing the right calibre of professional, the employer may only run one or two major 'institutional' ads a year for that type of position.

■ Cross-check the categories. Don't rely solely on those ads seeking your specific job title. For example, let's say you are a graphic artist looking for a job in advertising. You should flag all advertising or public relations agencies with any kind of need. If they are actively taking on staff at the moment, logic will tell you that their employment needs are not restricted to that particular title.

If you are writing as the result of a newspaper advertisement, you should mention both the publication and the date. Do not abbreviate 'advertisement' to 'ad' unless space demands, and remember to underline or italicize the publication's title:

'I read your advertisement in the Daily News _on 6 October and, after researching your company, felt I had to write ...'_

_'I am responding to your recent advertisement offering the opportunity to get involved with _____.'_

'In re: Your advertisement in the Yorkshire Post _on the 8th of November. As you will notice, my entire background matches your requirements.'_

'Your notice regarding a _____ in _____ caught my eye, and your company name caught my attention.'

'This letter and attached CV are in response to your advertisement in _____.'

Networking

Networking is one of those dreadful words from the 1970s that unfortunately is so entrenched we might as well learn to live with it. Strip the hyperbole and it just means communicating with everyone you can get hold of – professional colleagues, academic peers and personal contacts – whether you know them well or not.

I must admit my attitude towards networking among professional colleagues and personal friends has undergone a change. In earlier times I pooh-poohed the idea as a cop-out employed by the weak-willed. I said the only way to go was to bite the bullet, pick up the telephone, and make contact. This is still the fastest and most effective way. But I now recognize that for a job search to be most effective, direct mail has an important part to play. Even so, I still harbour fears that someone, once comfortable with networking among old friends, will unconsciously derail a job search by ignoring other and possibly more fruitful avenues of exploration for job opportunities. You would be wise to harbour the same fears; an effective job search is more than writing to old cronies and gossiping with them on the telephone.

What made me change my opinion? I consciously began to track my responses to requests for job hunting assistance.

To those requests from people I didn't know, I asked for a CV. If I received it in good time with a thoughtfully prepared accompanying letter, I would give that person help if I could.

To those requests from people with an introduction from someone I liked and respected, I gave time and consideration and, wherever possible, assistance.

To those requests from friends, people I had worked with at one time and *who had kept in touch* since we had worked together, I stopped everything and went through my address book. I provided leads, made calls on their behalf, and insisted they keep in touch. I also initiated follow-up calls myself on behalf of these people.

To those requests from people who regarded themselves as friends but who had not maintained contact, or who had only re-established contact when they wanted something, I looked through my address book once but for some reason was unable to find anything. I wished them the best of luck. 'Sorry I couldn't help you. If something comes to mind, I'll be sure to call.'

Nothing works like a personal recommendation from a fellow profes-sional – and you get that best by _being_ a fellow professional. It is no accident that successful people in all fields know each other – they helped each other get that way.

If you are going to use business colleagues and personal friends in your job search, don't mess up and do it half-heartedly. We live in a very mobile society, so you shouldn't restrict yourself to family, friends and colleagues just where you are looking. Everyone can help – even Aunt Matilda in Manila. Maybe she just happens to have had her cousin's wife's brother, who is a senior scientist at IBM, as her house guest for a month last summer and he is now forever in her debt for the holiday of a lifetime. Maybe not, but still, people know people, and they know people not just here but all over. Sit and think for a few minutes; you will be amazed at the people _you_ know all over the country. Every one of them has a similar network.

Here are some tips for writing letters asking for assistance. If you feel awkward writing a letter to certain contacts, use these guidelines as a basis for the telephone conversation you'll have instead.

1. Establish connectivity. Recall the last memorable contact you had or someone in common that you have both spoken to recently.

2. Tell them why you are writing: 'It's time for me to make a move; I just got laid off with a thousand others and I'm taking a couple of days to catch up with old friends.'

3. Ask for advice and guidance: 'Who do you think are the happening _____ companies today?' 'Could you take a look at my CV for me? I really need an objective opinion and I've always respected your view-point.' Don't ask specifically, 'Can you employ me?' or 'Can your company take me on?'

4. Don't rely on a contact with a particular company to get you into that company. Mount and execute your own plan of attack. No one has the same interest as you in putting bread on your table.

5. Let them know what you are ready to take on. They will invariably want to help, but you have to give them a framework within which to target their efforts.

6. Say you hope you'll get to see each other again soon or 'one of these days'. Plan on doing something together. Invite them over for drinks, dinner, or a barbecue.

7. When you do get help, say thank you. And if you get it verbally, follow it up in writing. The impression is indelible, and just might get you another lead.

8. You never know who your friends are. You will be surprised at how someone you always regarded as a real pal won't give you the time of day and how someone you never thought of as a friend will go beyond the call of duty for you.

9. Whether they help you or not, let them know when you get a job, and maintain contact in one form or another at least once a year. A career is for a long time. It might be next week or a decade from now when a group of managers (including one of your personal network) are talking about filling a new position and the first thing they will do is say 'Who do we know?' That could be you ... if you establish 'top of the mind awareness' now and maintain it.

If you are writing as the result of a referral, say so and quote the person's name if appropriate:

'Our mutual colleague John Stanovich felt my skills and abilities would be valuable to your company ...'

'The manager of your Ipswich branch, Pamela Bronson, has suggested I contact you regarding the opening for a _____.'

'I received your name from Henry Charles last week. I spoke to Mr Charles regarding career opportunities with _____, and he suggested I contact you. In case the CV he forwarded is caught up in the mail, I enclose another.'

'Arthur Gold, your office manager and my neighbour, thought I should contact you about the upcoming opening in your accounts department.'

Direct-Research Contacts

The Internet is now the most comprehensive job hunting resource. There are many Web sites that provide company profiles, and often you can e-mail the companies you're interested in right from their Web site. In addition to researching contacts, you can look up information on the status of the company you're interested in, do salary surveys, get advice on finding a job, and post your CV on online CV banks.

Most companies are also listed in one of the reference sources in your library. Take the time to do library research and you will discover job opportunities that 90 per cent of your professional competitors never dreamed existed.

Again, the reference librarian will be pleased to help you. Search each of the appropriate reference works for every company within the scope of your search that also falls within your geographic boundaries.

Your goal is to identify and build personalized dossiers on the companies in your chosen geographic area. Do not be judgemental about what and who they might appear to be: you are fishing for possible job openings, so cast your net wide and list them all. Only if you present yourself as a candidate for all available opportunities in your geographic area of search is there any realistic chance of landing the best possible opportunity.

Unfortunately, no single reference work is ever complete. Their very size and scope mean that most are at least a little out of date at publication time. Also, no single reference work lists every company. Because you don't know what company has the very best job for you, you need to research as many businesses in your area as possible, and therefore you will have to look through numerous reference books.

Copy all the relevant information for each company. You'll want to include the names of the company's CEO and chairman of the board, a description of the company's services and/or products, the size of the company, and the locations of its various branches. Of course, if you find other interesting information, copy it down, by all means. For instance, you might come across information on growth or shrinkage in a particular area of a company; or you might read about recent acquisitions the company has made. Write it all down.

All this information will help you target potential employers and stand out in different ways. Your knowledge will create a favourable impression when you first contact the company; that you made an effort is noticed and sets you apart from other applicants who don't bother. The combination says that you respect the company, the opportunity and the interviewer; combined, these perceptions help say that you are a different quality of job candidate.

All your efforts have an obvious short-term value in helping you with job interviews and offers. Who would *you* interview and subsequently employ? The person who knows nothing about your company, or the person who knows everything and is enthusiastic about it?

Your efforts also have value in the long term, because you are building a personalized reference work of your industry/speciality/profession that will help you throughout your career whenever you wish to make a job change.

Purchasing Mailing Lists

Posting your CV online is now widely available, but purchasing mailing lists from professional mailing list companies can also be cheap and effective. Chances are there is a mailing list of exactly the kinds of movers and shakers you want to work for. These lists can be broken down for you by title, geography, postcode – all sorts of ways. They are affordable, too. To contact a broker, just look in your *Yellow Pages* under 'mailing list brokers/ compilers'.

As we have noted, even the most up-to-date lists and directories are out of date by the time they get to you, so it is a good investment of time to call and verify that Joe Bloggs, Head of Engineering, is still there. Apart from the obvious goal of sending mail to the right person, if Joe is no longer there you may be able to find out where he went. If so, you'll have uncovered another opportunity for yourself.

(Note: Mailing lists can be effective, but be sure to read the envelopes section in Chapter 5 before you purchase preprinted mailing labels.)

Associations

You're a member of an appropriate professional association, aren't you? Of course you are – or, if not, you will want to invest in membership just as soon as humanly possible. You don't know of an appropriate association? Your local librarian will be able to point you to directories of associations, or you could look on the Internet.

When you join an association, you get a membership list to use to network amongst your peers. This is the modern-day equivalent of the 'old boy' and 'old girl' networks. Also, for a nominal sum you can often pick up a preprinted mailing list or the same on disk.

Alumni/ae Associations

Many schools and colleges have an active alumni/ae association. The mailing list you can obtain from this source can vary from just names to names and occupations and (sometimes) names of employers. Being a fellow alumni/ae probably gives you a claim to 60 seconds of attention. Nearly every working alumni/ae could be worthy of a networking letter (just check through the examples) and a follow-up call. Never ever underestimate the power of 'the old school tie'.

Recruitment Agencies

(This section is taken from *Your Job Search Made Easy*, 3rd edn, by Mark Parkinson, published by Kogan Page.)

In most situations indirect applications involve approaching a recruitment agency that deals with your job area. You'll find plenty advertised in the *Yellow Pages* and newspapers. Professional agencies will invite you to call and discuss the sort of job you would like, and your circumstances, skills and abilities. They may give you some tests or exercises to complete. These are designed to find out more about the sorts of job that would suit you and what you are like as a person. If you're dealing with a professional agency, they will then describe the sorts of company they work with, and the vacancies they have on their books. After the first meeting they will send your details to the most likely companies and arrange inteviews on your behalf. This means that you don't have to contact potential employers directly.

The problem is that agencies are not impartial since they make their money out of their commercial clients. This means that they are unlikely ever to say anything bad about them. In view of this you need to consider a little quality control. Try these checks:

- How is the first meeting conducted?
- Is it thorough and professional?
- Do they appear to care about you as an individual?
- Do you feel comfortable asking questions?
- Can they answer your questions?
- Do they assess your needs accurately?
- Do they use plain English or is it all jargon?
- How hard do they try?
- Do they approach just one company or lots of them?
- Do they approach the companies you suggest?
- If you have an unsuccessful interview, do they find out why?
- Do they keep you up to date with progress?

If the agency doesn't measure up, try another one: after all, it's your career that is at stake. Also remember to visit your local Jobcentre, which can help you to find local jobs and arrange interviews. Since Jobcentres are non-profit making the advice given will be independent and unbiased.

Business Magazines

There are a number of uses here. The articles about interesting companies can alert you to growth opportunities, and the articles themselves can be mentioned in your job search letter. Most professional trade magazines rely more or less on the contributions of industry professionals. So articles bylined by John Brown, CEO of Openings at ABC Furnaces, could go into a little dossier for strictly targeted mailings. It's also a good idea to enclose the article with your letter. These mailings to sometime authors can be tremendously rewarding. Writing is hard, and writers have egos of mythical proportions (just ask my editor). A little flattery can go a long way.

By the same token, you can write to people who are quoted in articles. It's great to see your name in print; in fact there is only one thing better, and that is hearing that someone *else* saw your name in print and now thinks you're a genius. (Of course, you should bear in mind that most of these magazines also carry a recruitment section.)

These ideas are just some of the many unusual and effective ways to introduce yourself to companies. Browse through all of the sample letters in Chapter 8 to uncover other effective ideas.

Mass Mailings and You

Your first effort with a job search letter is to find an individual to whom you can address it. As noted earlier, 'Sir/Madam,' or 'To whom it may concern' says you don't care enough about the company to find out a name – they will pay more attention to the candidates who do. A name shows you have focus and guarantees that a specific individual will open and read your letter. You also have someone to ask for by name when you do your follow-up – important when you are interview hunting.

Must you send out hundreds or even thousands of letters in the coming weeks? I spoke to a woman on a phone-in TV show recently who had 'done everything and still not got a job.' She explained how she had sent out almost 300 letters and still wasn't employed. I asked her several questions that elicited some revealing facts. She had been job hunting for almost two years (that equals two or three letters a week), and there were, conservatively, 3,000 companies she could work for. (That equals a single approach with no follow-up to only one in 10 potential employers.) Two employer contacts a week will not get you back to work – or even on track. Only if you approach and establish communication with every possible employer and follow up properly will you create the maximum opportunity for yourself.

In the world of headhunters the statistical average is 700 contacts between offers and acceptances. These are averages of professionals representing only the most desirable jobs and job candidates to each other. When I hear the oft-quoted statements that it takes a white collar worker about eight months to get a job nowadays, I have a feeling those 700 or so contacts are being spread out needlessly. If you approach the job search in a professional manner, the way executive search professionals and recruitment agencies approach their work, you can be happily installed on the next rung of your career ladder within a few weeks or months.

I am not recommending that you immediately make up a list of 700 companies and mail letters to them today. That isn't the answer. Your campaign needs strategy. While every job-hunting campaign is unique, you will want to maintain a balance between the *number* of letters you send out on a daily and weekly basis and the *kinds* of letters you send out.

The key is to send out a balanced mailing representing all the different types of leads, and to send them out regularly and in a volume that will allow you to make follow-up calls. There are many headhunters who manage their time so well that they average over 50 calls a day, year in and year out. While you may aim at building your call volume up to this number, I recommend that you start out with more modest goals.

To start the campaign:

Source	Number of Letters Per Day
Internet job postings	10
Newspaper ads	10
Networking (associations, alumni/ae, colleagues)	10 (5 to friends, 5 to professional colleagues)
Direct-research contacts (online searches, reference works, magazines, etc)	10
Headhunters	10

Do You Need to Compose More Than One Letter?

Almost certainly. There is a case for all of us having letters and CVs in more than one format. The key is to do each variation once and do it right; and that, as we have seen, means keeping your work comprehensively backed up on disk. This way, even for future job searches, the legwork will already be done, and you'll be ready regardless of when opportunity or necessity comes knocking.

In fact, you may find it valuable to send upwards of half a dozen contact letters to any given company, to ensure that they know you are available. To illustrate this, let's say you are a young engineer desirous of gaining employment with Last Chance Electronics. It is well within the bounds of reason that you would mail job search or broadcast letters to any or all of the following people, with each letter addressed by name to minimize its chances of going straight into the waste-paper basket:

- Company Chairman

- CEO of Engineering

- Chief Engineer

- Engineering Design Manager
- Head of Human Resources
- Technical Engineering Recruitment Manager
- Technical Recruiter

The Plan

A professionally organized and conducted campaign will proceed on one of two plans of attack. Both of these plans should have an e-mail and traditional 'snail mail' dimension. So when I talk about 'mail' and 'mail campaign', understand it to embrace both communication mediums.

Approach 1

A carefully targeted approach to a select group of companies. You will have first identified these 'super-desirable' places to work as you researched your long list of potential employers. You will continue to add to this primary target list as you unearth fresh opportunities in your day-to-day research efforts. In this instance you have two choices:

1. Mail to everyone at once, remembering that the letters have to be personalized and followed up appropriately.

2. Start your mailings off with one to a line manager and one to a contact in human resources. Follow up in a few days and repeat the process to other names on your hit list.

With the e-mail dimension of your campaign, you can bookmark target companies and check in on their openings on an ongoing basis.

Approach 2

A carpet-bombing strategy designed to reach every possible employer on the basis that you won't know what opportunities there are unless you find out. (Here, too, you must personalize and follow up appropriately.)

Begin with a mailing to one or two contacts within the company and then repeat the mailings to other contacts when your initial follow-up calls result in referrals or dead ends. Remember, just because Harry in engineering says there are no openings in the company, that's not necessarily the case; always find out for yourself. Even if he doesn't have a need himself, any contact could know the person who is just dying to meet you.

Once you have received some responses to your mailings and scheduled interviews, your emphasis will change. Those contacts and interviews will require follow-up letters and conversations. You will be preparing for interviews.

This is exactly the point where most job hunts stall. We get so excited about the interview activity we convince ourselves that 'This will be the offer.' The headhunters have a saying, 'The offer that can't fail always will.' What happens is that the offer doesn't materialize, and we are left with absolutely no interview activity. We let the interview funnel empty itself.

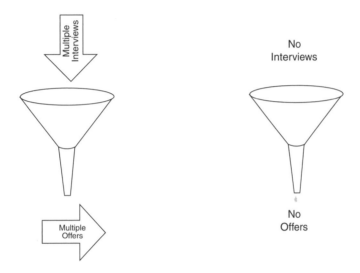

The more letters you send out, the more follow-up calls you can make to schedule interviews. The more interviews you get, the better you feel and the better you get at being interviewed. The better you get at being interviewed, the more offers you get.

So no matter how good things look, continue the campaign – maintain activity with those companies with which you are in negotiation. You must also maintain your marketing schedule. The daily plan now looks like this:

Source	Number of Letters Per Day
Internet job postings	5
Newspaper ads	5
Networking (associations, alumni/ae, colleagues)	5
Direct-research contacts (online searches, reference work, magazines, etc)	5
Headhunters	5
Follow-up letters and calls	15–20

Small but consistent mailings have many benefits. The balance you maintain is important, because most job hunters are tempted simply to send the easy letters and make the easy calls (ie, network with old friends). Doing this will knock your job search off balance.

Even when an offer is pending, keep plugging, and by 'pending' I include all variations on 'Harry, you've got the job and you can start Monday; the offer letter is in the mail'. Yeah, just like the cheque in the proverb. Never accept the 'yes' until you have it in writing, have started work, and the first pay cheque has cleared at the bank! Until then, keep your momentum building.

Following Up: A Cautionary Tale

In theory, your perfect letter will generate a 100 per cent response. But there is no perfect letter, and this is a less-than-perfect world. Although you will get calls from your mailing, if you sit there like Buddha waiting for the world to beat a path to your door, you may wait a long time.

Not long ago a pal of mine put a two-line ad in the local paper for a programmer analyst. By Wednesday of the following week he had received over a hundred responses. Ten days later he was still ploughing through them when he received a follow-up call (the only one he did receive) from one of the ad respondents. The job hunter was in the office within two hours, returned the following morning, and was employed by lunchtime.

The candidate's paperwork was simply languishing there in the pile waiting to be discovered. The follow-up phone call got it discovered. The call made the interviewer sort through the enormous pile of paper, pull out the letter and CV, and act on it. Follow-up calls work.

You'll notice that many letters in Chapter 8 mention that they will follow up with a phone call. This allows the writer to explain to any inquisitive receptionist that Joe Bloggs is 'expecting my call' or that it is 'personal'.

I find it surprising that so many professionals are nervous about calling a fellow professional on the phone and talking about what they do for a living. To help reduce any nervousness, understand that there is an unwritten professional credo shared by the vast majority of successful professional people: you should always help another if it isn't going to hurt you in the process.

If you are not already successful in management, you need to know the principle outlined in my management books *Hiring the Best* and *Keeping the Best*: 'The first tenet of management is getting work done through others'. A manager's success is truly based on this single idea. Managers are always on the lookout for competent professionals in their field for today and tomorrow. In fact, the best managers maintain a private file of great professionals they can't use today but want to keep available. I know of someone who got a job as a result of a letter retained in these files. She got the interview (and the job) from the broadcast letter she'd sent eight years earlier.

No manager will take offence at a call from a competent fellow professional.

To ensure that you keep track of the contacts you have made and the results of the follow-up phone calls, create a Contact Tracker.

How to Use the Contact Tracker

I recommend that you make your own Contact Tracker on a spreadsheet program. Create columns for the company name, telephone number, e-mail address and contact name. A mailing today will allow you to have a follow-up plan set and ready to go at the appropriate time. As a rule of thumb, a mailing sent today is ripe for follow-up four to eight days from now. Any sooner and you can't be sure it has arrived; much later and it may already have been lost or been passed on. In addition to your Contact Tracker, it may be helpful to use your computer address book to keep track of who you contact.

You will know that your job search is on track when you are filling in more contacts every day as a result of a mailing, and creating a second Contact Tracker as a result of your follow-up calls.

If you follow the advice in this book, you will get interviews. If you follow the advice in *Resumes That Knock 'em Dead* and *Knock 'em Dead*, you will get multiple job offers. When you get your first job offer, you will want to read the section on multiple offers in Knock 'em Dead, which will show you how to turn many of these contacts into additional interviews and competitive offers.

Recently I spoke to a man on a radio phone-in show who had been out of work for some months. He had bought the books and followed my advice to the letter and had generated four job offers in only five weeks. I have lost count of the number of similar encounters I've had over the years. Follow my advice in letter and spirit and the same good fortune can be yours. After all, good fortune is really only the intersection of opportunity, preparation and effort.

7

Using the Internet and Creating Electronic Job Search Letters

The Internet has established itself as a useful and vital job search tool. Here's the lowdown on everything you need to know to get online effectively and with results!

How the Internet Can Help in Your Job Hunt

The Internet can be of great assistance in your job hunt. It offers you an array of opportunities and chances to get your CV on the desks of thousands of companies and recruiters. It will not, however, effectively replace your other job-hunting activities. You need to utilize it as one of the many useful weapons already in your job-hunting arsenal. A job search becomes more effective when you widen its geographic scope, and the Internet easily allows you to access numerous job openings in major metropolitan areas. The usefulness of an Internet search diminishes when you are only looking for jobs in your immediate area. Nevertheless, online searches can still provide valuable information about local opportunities as well.

The Internet can be intimidating – ask anyone who has done an online search for a lost college friend or looked for cheap air fare on the very day of his or her flight. Job-hunting is challenging enough work in its own right, why complicate matters by learning new technologies that may not apply to your particular needs? Can the Internet really help you, or is it only for techies?

This chapter focuses on giving you the facts and the most effective techniques in online job-hunting. Knowing these facts, you can decide on the merits of Internet searches for yourself.

The vast majority of companies are now using their Web sites as recruiting portals. From the corporate perspective, Internet recruitment serves a dual purpose: their personnel openings are posted on the Web to attract candidates, and the technologically challenged are screened out by virtue of default.

How can the Internet benefit your job search? It allows you to:

- Create customized electronic documents and communicate with potential employers and recruiters within seconds.

- Find job openings through job banks and employers' job sites.

- Have potential employers find you, whether you are currently looking for a position or just managing your career growth opportunities.

- Do research on companies, potential employers and your industry.

- Make better career and life decisions through the use of career tools and online services.

Anyone can use the Web to find opportunities for climbing the corporate ladder. The Internet offers you access to millions of job openings, and tens of thousands of companies and recruiters. You'll be able to communicate your qualifications to the world in minutes, resulting in more responses; you can post your CV on the Internet so that companies and recruiters can find you; and you'll have access to more information about prospective employers, making you a better-informed candidate.

What You Need to Start an Online Job Search

You need computer access from outside the workplace. Using your office computer for writing your CV, sending out e-mails, or surfing the net for job listings is the Internet equivalent of stealing company stationery and postage stamps. Studies show that 50 per cent of all companies read their employees' e-mail and/or track their Internet usage. Some companies have even implemented schemes offering a 'finders' fee' if someone locates a staff member's CV online. Originating primarily in the high-tech industries, this practice seems to be on the rise in industries across the board. Don't ignore this warning because you feel your boss is computer illiterate, too stupid to catch you, or too trusting to snoop. Almost all companies are using the Internet for recruitment purposes; someone in Human Resources could accidentally stumble across your online CV, which lists the company you're currently working for. Moreover, tracking software allows your employer to spy on company computer usage, and it is legal for them do so. Bottom line: do not use an employer's computer or e-mail address for job-searching activities.

Online Privacy and Organization

Personal privacy and confidentiality become serious issues when you use the Internet for the purposes of job-hunting and CV distribution. It's a good news/bad news situation: with the ease of electronic document distribution comes the fear of prying eyes. So take precautions to protect your privacy.

If you have Internet access at home, it is probably through a local ISP (internet service provider). These accounts typically come with one e-mail address, and most people set that up for family use. This should not be your job search e-mail address. You need to set up a separate online identity and maintain it exclusively for your job search.

As your experience broadens, your education and professional experience will allow you to pursue a number of different jobs. Therefore, you have the option of creating multiple professional identities online. Setting up separate e-mail accounts for each of these career-specific identities will allow you to keep things organized by job classification, giving more focus to your search and allowing you to effectively manage your job-hunting activities.

Privacy Is a Concern for Everyone

Don't include too much personal information in an online CV. It could allow unscrupulous people to use your personal or professional identity for their own purposes. Posting your home phone number or address on the Internet attracts junk mail and telemarketing calls.

Anyone who has an e-mail account is familiar with junk e-mail, commonly referred to as 'spam'. Reverse spamming is when an electronic 'spider' grabs your personal information, e-mail address, or CV, then redistributes it to other sites or a third party. An electronic spider is a programmed tool that searches the Internet for certain types of information the 'spider owner' specifies. Don't be afraid to use the Internet in your job search, but be aware that the information that you post is readily available to other users. Be careful about the type of information and the amount of personal data you make electronically available.

When using a free e-mail account, handling junk mail is an expected inconvenience you must tolerate for the service. Identity fraud, however, is a far more serious complication that can potentially arise in free e-mail usage. You put your professional identity at risk when listing professional licences or certificate numbers on your CV – so don't do it, ever! In addition, dates of birth, driver's licence numbers and National Insurance numbers should never be included on electronic CVs. With that information alone, someone could steal your identity and ruin your personal or professional credibility.

Rules to Protect Your Online Privacy

Here are some general guidelines for making online job sites and CV banks work *for* you rather than *against* you:

- Look at the site's privacy statement. Read it carefully to understand the extent of protection afforded to personal information. Even without guarantees, this is a security starting point.

- Only post your CV to sites that protect their CV bank with a password (this is the best prevention against those spiders). Password protection means that the site electronically screens all visitors. This helps to ensure that only credible employers and recruiters have access to your CV.

- Know who owns and operates the site. The owner's contact information should be available. If they are unwilling to share their identity with you, don't share yours either.

- You must be able to update, edit and remove your posted CV, along with any other personal information whenever you choose.

- Blocked CV bank services are services that supposedly allow you to block access to your information from specifically unwanted viewers, such as a current employer. Do not trust these services to actually do so. These sites are not foolproof, so only post items that you don't need blocked.

- If you decide to build and create your own Web site to post your CV and work samples, password-protect it.

- Never put your National Insurance number, driver's licence number or professional licence number on your CV in any format.

- Do not use your company e-mail address, computer, or Internet lines to search for jobs or to access your private e-mail account.

Free E-mail Accounts

There are dozens of sites that offer free e-mail accounts that take only minutes to set up. While many personal interest sites offering free accounts exist, remember that your career e-mail address shouldn't contain any personal information. *Martin@match.com* reveals too much personal information, and isn't appropriate for professional use. You want to create a professional, eye-catching image right from the start; take time in selecting your professional e-mail service and user names.

As an example of the process, let's create a new identity for a fictional job search candidate, Susan O'Malley, using Hotmail. Go to *www.hotmail.com*, and then select the 'Sign Up' icon on the front page of the site. That will link you to a page requesting a user profile. When you complete the profile, you will be directed to the site user agreement. This explains user rules and the site's privacy policy. Read this information carefully; you have to accept the terms of the agreement before your address becomes active. Stick with the larger, more public firms, because they tend to be more reliable and honourable about such terms. Typically, public sites offer paid upgrades to your new account that allow you more control over your e-mail address. Upgrades are unnecessary if you limit the number of messages stored in your mailbox at any given time, or don't care to pay to limit spam.

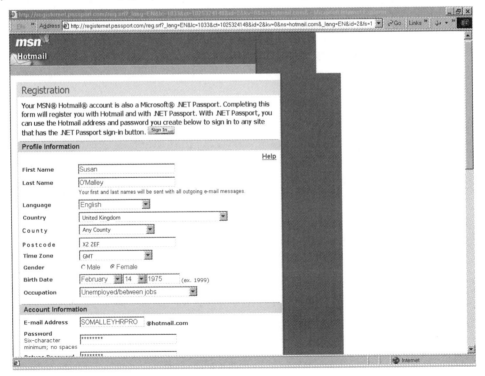

Account signup

You will notice that I chose a professional user name for Susan: SOMAL-LEYHRPRO – this gives her the e-mail address *somalleyhrpro@hotmail.com.* Remember: this account is set up strictly for job search purposes. An appropriately named professional e-mail like this will grab the attention of prospective employers.

Should you run into a situation where the user name you want is not available, choose your alternatives wisely. Most sites will make suggestions, usually by adding numbers to the end of the user name. This is not appropriate for job-hunting and career management needs. You do not want to be confused with *jsmith118@hotmail.com* when you are assigned the name *jsmith119@hotmail.com,* nor do you want to choose a number that could easily be mistaken for your year of birth. Instead, make it a career-related screen name as we did for Susan.

How to Organize Your Job-Hunting E-mail Account

For those of you planning to use public or shared computers, free accounts such as this one offer a nice security feature at the front door – provided you utilize it. Susan activated the highest level of security by clicking on the 'Public/shared computer' button. At this increased level of security, Susan will be asked for her user name and password whenever she attempts to enter her account from any computer. If Susan always uses her home or private computer, the 'Neither' or the 'Keep me signed in' option assumes that every time her Web browser links to Hotmail, she is identified as the user and is automatically logged in. This also allows her to keep her job search secure on her family computer. For your own safety, emulate Susan and set up your account at the highest security level possible.

Whether you use Hotmail, Yahoo!, Outlook, or some other major e-mail program, all of them allow you to create and manage folders. (Do you see the buttons for 'Create Folder' and 'Manage Folders' in the figures below?) Think of these as the electronic equivalent of paper folders and filing cabinets. What folders do you need? Let's start with the two major sites where Susan will be posting her CV and searching for jobs: Monster.com and SHRM.org (the Society for Human Resource Management Web site). Both of these sites offer job delivery services, so when she signs up at either of them using her new e-mail account, she is quickly able to review jobs and file those she wants to save.

Susan will also create a folder for leads. As the leads mature into communication and contact with specific companies and recruiters, she can create specific folders for them. To get started, Susan's new e-mail account looks like this:

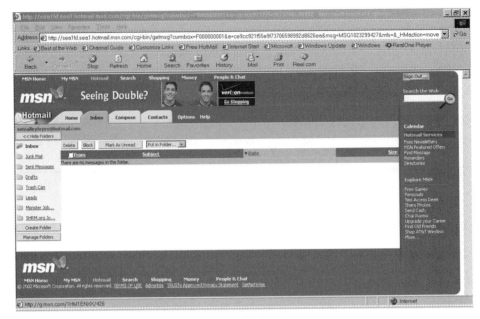

The new e-mail account

Organization does not end there. It is crucial to your long-term ability to manage your career that you are constantly and consistently building a contact manager for job prospects. This applies both to companies you might want to work for, and for contacts within recruiting firms. Follow Susan's example and you will be 10 steps ahead of the game when you next need to make a strategic career move.

Take another look at the previous screen shot, only this time look up to the right, above the messages. Locate the tab in the middle of the screen labelled 'Address Book'. This tab sends you to another screen, where you are given additional options. These options allow you to send e-mail, view and edit messages, delete e-mail, and, most importantly for your organizational efforts: create a new address book.

In creating new address books, you want to organize groups of addresses, not just add individual ones. Each 'group' will contain a separate set or group of addresses, tailored to specific audiences for current or future job searches. Typically, these groups fall into three categories: companies, recruiters and networking prospects/professional colleagues. By creating an address book group for each of these categories, you create a database for your working life.

Additions to these groups needn't be based on direct contact, interviews, or job offers. If you see a recruiter within an industry of interest, put that address in the recruiter book. If you find a company in your geographic area or professional field, put that address in the company book. By doing this regularly, you create a vehicle for launching a massive career blitz whenever

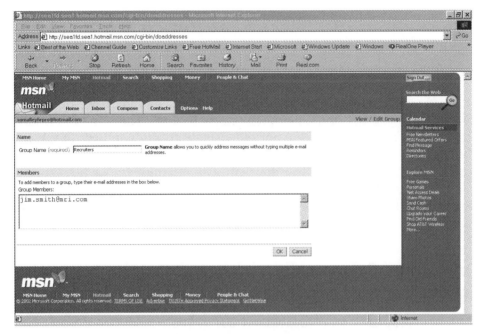

Address book groups

the need arises. Organize yourself now, and the information you collect along the way can be used throughout your entire working life. You'll have an enormous database loaded and ready to go!

Job Search Letters and Online Job-Hunting

A great CV is critical to job search success, but it will remain unread without a dynamite letter to go with it. In the electronic world, your job search letter is embedded in the e-mail message preceding your CV, and it should include an attention grabbing e-mail subject line.

The Internet and the subsequent growth of the electronic recruitment process have been both a blessing and a curse for corporate recruiters. Although electronic recruitment can be much more efficient for them in many ways, it tends to yield more responses from a wider range of candidates. This creates a time-management challenge for corporations and recruiters who must review the avalanche of CVs the medium generates. This has resulted in a dramatic growth in CV software capable of scanning CV databases by keywords.

With traditionally mailed CVs, a powerful job search letter separates a job hunter from the crowd. This is equally applicable with an electronic version. As is the case for your electronic CV, your electronic job search letter needs to contain three musts:

1. It must have the right key words.

2. It must be scannable.

3. It must be transmittable over the Web via e-mail.

Think of your job search letter as an electronic talent agent, the opening act for your CV. The two must complement each other. The topic of electronic distribution is covered more comprehensively in my companion CV book *The Ultimate CV Book.* Both play a crucial role in the successful electronic job search. No matter how well written job search letters are, or how sophisticated your electronic approaches become, an ineffectively presented CV (either from keyword or compatibility failures) will result in a job-hunting dead end.

Differences Between Electronic and Paper Job Search Letters

Modern workplaces tend to demand 60+ hours weekly from busy, multitasking employees. I've spoken to corporate executives who base their decision on whether to listen to voice mail messages on the first 10 words recorded. Your electronic job search letter competes for the attention of this same audience.

E-mail communications are treated in a similar fashion. Daily, the amount of e-mail traffic grows exponentially. Most professionals receive dozens, sometimes hundreds, of messages per day. Hit your main points quickly, or you will lose the reader's attention. A good e-mail subject line determines what attention your CV and job search letter receive. If the first two sentences don't succinctly state your purpose and grab their attention, they'll have little reason for wasting any more precious time on the rest of your message.

Hard copy cover letters usually consist of three to five carefully constructed paragraphs. Very rarely should they exceed one full page; in most cases, a second page simply won't get read. They should strategically emphasize, or re-emphasize, points made in your CV. They can also be used to customize applications for specific positions, or to address issues not covered in your CV.

Electronic job search letters need to be even shorter and more concise than those on paper. Just as you would limit a paper job search letter to one page, you should keep an electronic job search letter to one screen view (three to five sentences at most). Don't force the readers to scroll down to see the rest of the letter – chances are they won't do it. Sound too short? Not in cyberland. Be sure to use keywords highlighting your potential and past career accomplishments.

Before discussing formatting, let's take a minute to focus on job search letter content issues. We've established the fact that electronic job search letters need to be short. Their task is to quickly tell the recipient why the message is being sent and give them a reason to read the CV. Review the samples below. Look for the ways in which these letters build bridges between writers and readers, use keywords, make points about the writers' suitability for the positions, and then request next step information.

Sample 1

I was excited to see your opening for a Financial Analyst (job 1854) on the ABCJob.com Web site. As my attached CV demonstrates, the position is a perfect match for my payroll, general ledger and accounts receivable experience. I welcome the opportunity to discuss my skills and your job requirements in greater detail. I will follow up with you next week.

Sample 2

While browsing the jobs database on the MedZilla.com Web site, I was intrigued by your Regional Sales Manager job posting (MZ - wj25508). Although I am currently employed by one of your competitors, I have kept my eyes open for an opportunity to join your organization. Over the past year I have: ■ Built a sales force of 7 reps ■ Exceeded my quota-growing revenue to £2.3 million ■ Implemented a customer service plan that successfully retains clients.

Please review my attached CV and contact me confidentially to schedule a time for us to meet.

Sample 3

It was great meeting you on Monday for lunch. I enjoyed sharing ideas with a fellow association member and, as you suggested, I have attached a copy of my current CV. Since our meeting I have given more thought to your company goals and believe they are closely related to my skill set and career objectives. If I don't hear from you this week, I will call you no later than next week to schedule a time when we can continue our conversation.

Sample 4

Your colleague Bill Jacobson suggested that I send you my CV. He mentioned that your department is looking for a Database Administrator with experience in Intranet implementation and management. As my attached CV demonstrates, I have done that type of work for six years with a regional organization on a platform of 15,000 users. I welcome the opportunity to discuss your specific projects and explore the possibility of joining your team.

Sample 5

Although I am currently employed by one of your major competitors, I must admit that I was captivated by your company's mission statement when I visited your Web site. I found your company philosophy regarding the care of elderly people to be of significant interest to me as both a Healthcare Professional of 17 years and the child of aged parents. Your dedication of resources within assisted care facilities and laboratory growth practices not only piqued my interest but are also, as my attached CV indicates, precisely my area of expertise. With significant experience in an area of such importance to your firm, I look forward to the opportunity to discuss available positions.

Sample 6

A former colleague of mine, Diane Johnson, recommended your recruiting firm to me as you recently assisted her in a career transition. I understand that your firm specializes in the consumer products industry, with particular attention to sales, marketing and business development vacancies. As a Marketing Director with 12 years of experience in consumer products, I have:

- *doubled revenues in just 18 months;*
- *introduced a new product which captured a 78% market share;*
- *successfully managed a £5 million ad budget.*

I have included my CV for your review and will call you next week to discuss any openings for which your firm is currently conducting searches.

The content of each of these electronic job search letter samples follows a similar format. They all accomplish three things:

- They identify why you are sending your CV.
- They identify why the reader should read the CV.
- They ask for the interview or next contact.

Let's examine each of these points more closely:

Identify why you made contact: You probably initiated contact because of a job posting, a colleague, or because your research identified them as a potential employer or suitable recruiting firm. Just state the reason and tell the reader you see a match. When submitting because of a job posting, always indicate the job title or job number if there is one. Likewise, if a friend, associate, or colleague initiated the contact, clearly state their name and your connection. If you found the opening through Internet research, state that as well.

Give them a reason to read your CV: Quickly and concisely identify why you believe you are a match. Read the job posting again and then repeat the keywords that you share with it. If appropriate, explain the reason why your mutual acquaintance or colleague referred you and follow on by stating your experience and skill sets. This is your chance to whet the reader's appetite. If you are currently employed by, or have worked for a competitor, say it here – many companies seek the expertise of their competitors, and love to lure employees away from them.

Ask for the next step: Wrap up this brief but powerful communication by suggesting a meeting, phone call, or interview. Go ahead and state that you will follow-up, especially if you are currently employed and confidentiality could be an issue. But if you say you are going to follow-up, you must make time to do it.

The Need for Multiple Electronic Job Search Letters

You will be sending your CV and job search letter in response to many different situations, and one letter can't fit all possible scenarios. To maximize effectiveness, you will have to tailor your job search letters to specific audiences. Addressees may include:

1. Companies and recruiters in response to online job postings.

2. Companies you've found from research, newspapers, trade publications and the Internet.

3. Recruiters and the all-important headhunters.

4. Friends and professional colleagues as a means of networking and staying in touch professionally.

When sending CVs to each of these types of contacts, slightly different job search letters will be required. You'll find lots of examples to emulate and customize later in this book. Now that you understand the content strategy of electronic job search letters, it is time to write your own samples, and then translate them into an electronic format. My suggestion is that you compose job search letters using a word processing program, not in your e-mail folder. Even though you are most likely to send the letter via e-mail, it is best to compose it elsewhere and move it into e-mail when you're satisfied with the content.

Next, it is a good idea to create templates for a variety of job search letters. This allows you to quickly access and customize a job search letter for a specific prospective employer. In the long run, templates make you more time-efficient in your job-hunting campaign.

Let's address organization again, in this case specifically the organization of your job search documents. If you start now, you will stay organized throughout the job search. You'll create a lifelong career management database, allowing you to adapt your templates to specific future needs as worthwhile opportunities arise. Time spent organizing your own database now saves time and makes future searches easier and more effective.

Go to your 'My Documents' or 'My Briefcase' folder, then create a series of new folders for the various documents and relationships you will be building. This is what Susan's initial folder system looks like:

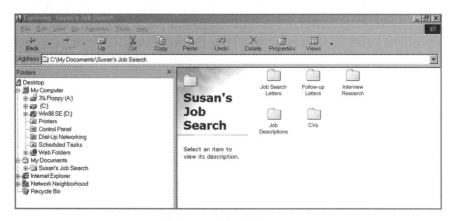

Job search folders

As you can see, she's created a separate section in the 'My Documents' folder, then created a series of subfolders for 'CVs', 'Job Search Letters', 'Job Descriptions', 'Follow-up Letters' and 'Interview Research'. She also reserves space for 'Job Offers' and 'Employment Contracts' folders to handle such responses when her job search gains momentum.

Remember, in each of these folders, you need to name documents appropriately; create additional subfolders like Susan's 'Text Job Search Letters' subfolder, which is embedded in the 'Job Search Letters' folder. Keep your electronic job search letters separate from paper versions. Get organized in advance, then you'll never worry about it again. At this point, you may have already written a few traditional job search letter drafts. These are a good place to start in building up your new folders, but always remember to apply the electronic rules and to address your 'hot points' succinctly.

A Scannable Job Search Letter

Companies scan and digitize almost all job search letters and CVs received, whether mailed or faxed paper copy, or formatted e-mail and attachments. Be careful about formatting and font issues in the organization process; you don't want your documents in an unreadable or odd-looking state when received.

As a general rule, don't use dark backgrounds, page borders, columns, excessive bold, underlining, italics, or fonts smaller than 10-point in e-mail documents. They may look good on hard copy, but they may not be scannable in that format; and it is all likely to get lost in e-mail formatting anyway. Avoiding such artistic touches saves composition time, giving you more time for other job search activities.

You should be focusing on the creation of effective e-mail job search letters and subject lines that grab the attention of human readers , bypassing the possibility of getting lost in the employer database maze. It's still a good idea to base your electronic job search letters on the formalized traditional job search letter, shortening and customizing them for the medium.

Make Sure Your Job Search Letters Are in the Correct Electronic Format

Let's revisit Susan O'Malley in the process of editing and shortening her traditional job search letter, and converting it to an ASCII or text-based document for her e-mail job searching use.

Susan's generic traditional job search letter is nicely formatted, matching the layout of her CV. At this point, the letter is one full page in length, listing a dozen bullet points regarding her skill set. Although not customized for any particular audience, the style is that of a traditional job search letter. It needs editing before it will be ready for e-mail use.

The first step is removing the parts of traditional job search letters that translate poorly into the electronic world. Unlike regular business letters, e-mail letters do not follow typical letter-writing protocols. For example, you would not include a header from the sender or the date: e-mail automatically acknowledges these aspects. Similarly, the addressee's mailing address, company name and title (if any) are automatically encoded by the process.

Begin your business e-mail messages with a simple salutation, followed by the person's name. Don't address the recipient on a first-name basis unless you are already familiar with them; use the same courtesy and respect you would in a hard copy version.

Always end your business e-mails stating your name and a brief summary of your contact information (confidential phone number or fax, mailing address, etc). Remove the enclosure indication, and state that the CV is *attached* (the correct term), or that it's pasted into the body of the e-mail per the recipient's preference.

The first edit of Susan's CV looks like this:

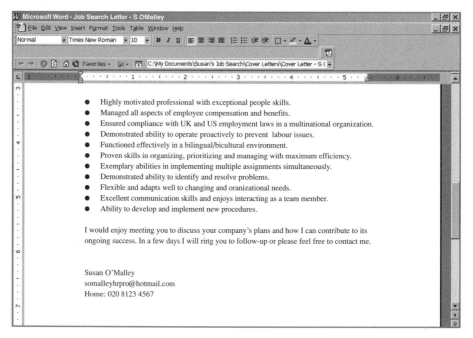

The first edit of the job search letter

Although this letter is still too long, it allows flexibility for specific tailoring. She can edit the bulleted list according to the requirements of any individual position she seeks. At this point, let's ignore the length issue to focus on format. If placed into the body of an e-mail message, this text would develop character and spacing problems. To avoid such problems, convert your job search letters to ASCII or a text-based document before pasting it into or attaching it to your e-mail. This is accomplished by following these simple steps.

Copy the entire document by choosing 'select all' from the 'edit' pull-down menu (or Cmd+A for Macintosh). Then, choose 'copy' from the 'edit' pull-down menu or Ctrl+C for Windows (Cmd+C for Macintosh).

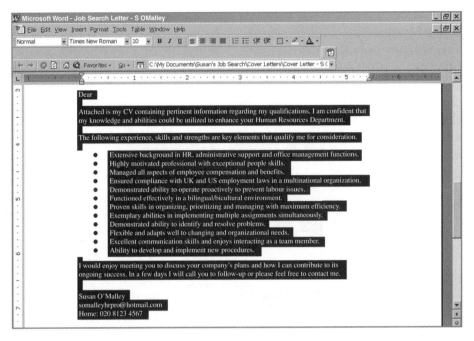

Selecting all text

Open a new document in your word processor. Set the margins to 60 characters per line, equating to 1.7 to 1.75 inch right and left margins. Or, you can count out 60 characters if that's easier for you.

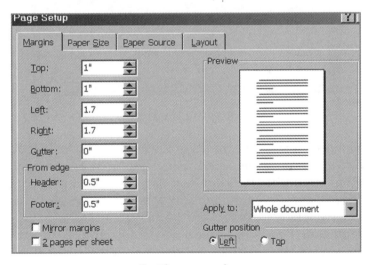

Setting margins

The number of characters in each line must be limited because electronic screens are limited to that viewing width, and this precludes text wrapping off the screen.

Next, paste the job search letter you just copied into this new document. Do that by choosing 'Paste' from the 'edit' pull-down menu or Ctrl+V for Windows (or Cmd+V for Macintosh). Initially, the documents still look very similar, but further necessary edits alter that. Typically, letters become longer as each line length is decreased.

Go back to the 'edit' pull-down menu, choosing 'select all' (Cmd+A for Macintosh). This allows you to change the font type and size. Select 'Font' from the 'Format' pull-down menu and change the font type to 'Times New Roman' or 'Courier'. Change the size to 12-point.

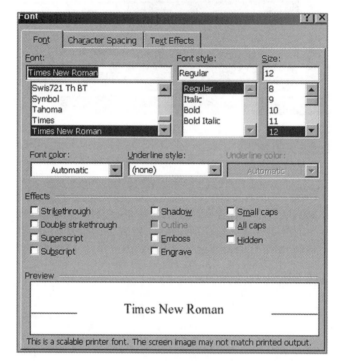

Changing the font

Notice the changes in the appearance of the letter here. We're still not done. This new document must be saved using the 'save as' command. It also requires further modification. Select 'text only' as your document type, then rename it. Let's name it 'O'Malley Text Job Search Letter 1', saving it in Susan's job search letter folder.

Pay close attention here: a message box will appear indicating that continuing will change your formatting. Answer 'yes' to continue at this prompt; you need to strip the formatting in order to create an ASCII or text-based document. Remember, you want to avoid all chances of character and spacing problems in your e-mail letter; sticking to a straight text-based document allows all readers to receive your message in the style you wish it viewed.

The document has lost many of its features and the spacing is totally altered. You need to spend some time proofreading this new document. Any tabs, tables or columns used in a formatted version wreak havoc in new text-based versions. In order to prevent wrapping or flowing issues, you need to remove empty spaces and tabs to make the document flush left.

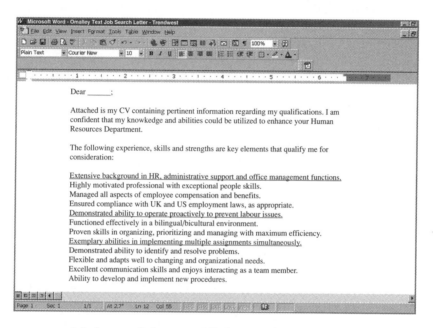

A job search letter with formatting removed

Since the bullets have disappeared in the translation, either adjust the spacing to create a new type of emphasis, or use characters on your keyboard such as * to replace the bullets. In addition, the bullet statements need to be shorter and more concise. If you allow statements to wrap to the next line, your electronic job search letters will be unappealing, less effective and too long. Save your document to protect all these changes. Keep in mind, this is a template. Once an actual contact or job opening has been identified, customization will be the next step.

How to Use the All-Important Subject Line of E-mail Effectively

The use of a powerful subject line can mean the difference between getting your CV read and being relegated to the HR CV database. When sending e-mail – not just job related e-mails, but all e-mails – it is only professional to provide a clear, concise and professional subject line. It allows the receiver to immediately know who you are and what you want.

The subject line of an e-mail containing your CV needs to be factual, professional and intriguing. The subject line you use is like the headline for a newspaper article, and can have the same effect on the audience – it will attract the reader or turn them off. The intent of your e-mail subject line must be to grab the reader and draw him or her into the body of the e-mail message and your CV. Do not use the subject line to state the obvious, like 'CV' or 'Jim Smith's CV'. Keep your audience in mind – just as you would when composing your job search letters and CV. What are they looking for?

If you are responding to a job posting, the job title and job posting number are necessary, but just a start. Combine this factual information with a little intrigue such as:

Job 6745 – Top Sales Professional Here
IT Manager – 7 yrs IT Consulting
Financial Analyst MB450 – CPA / MBA / 8 yrs exp
Benefits Consultant – Non-Profit Exp in London
Posting 2314 – Oxford Grad is interested
Referral from Tony Banks – Product Management Job

Remember, although you want to grab someone's attention, this is still a professional and serious topic – your career. Do not go overboard and use an overly aggressive subject line. Do not think you can trick someone into reading your CV by claiming to be an Oxbridge graduate when you are not. Not to mention the fact that because everyone gets so much junk mail, a whimsical subject line might land your CV right in the delete bin.

How to Customize and Send Your Electronic Job Search Letter and CV

Let's pull it all together and watch Susan, an HR professional, customize her electronic job search letter, pick an effective subject line, and send her CV to a potential employer.

Susan is looking for a job in the USA and has been using the Society for Human Resource Management career site (*www.shrg.org*) and has found an appealing position in sunny California. A vacation resort company is seeking a Regional HR Manager.

The job posting has requested that correspondence be sent in the following manner:

Qualified candidates send resume, salary history and cover letter to: jadariav@gourmetaward.com *or fax 555-555-1234.*

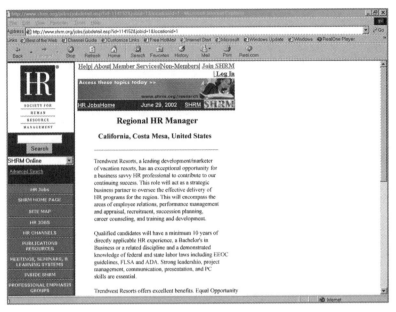

Job posting

Susan is going to e-mail and post her customized job search letter and electronic CV (resume) to this employer. Since the employer did not provide any additional direction, it is best if Susan attaches the CV to her e-mail message as well as pasting it into the body of the e-mail. Let's start by customizing her electronic job search letter template and then choose a strong subject line.

Since Susan was smart enough to get herself organized, she can quickly find her electronic letter template. By comparing this longer template to the actual job description, she can easily spot the 'hot points'. This position requires 10 years of experience and the job description indicates that knowledge of employment laws such as EEOC, FLSA and ADA are important. As Susan has studied and worked with both US and UK employment law in her job with a major multinational, and since she is interested in moving to California, this is a good match.

Susan has customized her letter template well: she stated why she is sending the e-mail, hit her 'hot points' to get the reader's attention, and asked for the follow-up. In fact, she even renamed the document to reflect the company she will be sending it to and saved it in her job search letter folder. Before closing this document, Susan needs to copy the entire letter by choosing 'select all' from the 'edit' pull-down menu (or Cmd+A for Macintosh) and then choosing 'copy' from the 'edit' pull-down menu or Ctrl+C for Windows (Cmd+C for Macintosh).

The next step is to create the e-mail, insert the job search letter, and attach the CV. Susan will go back to her newly established Hotmail account, enter her user name and password, and create a new message by choosing

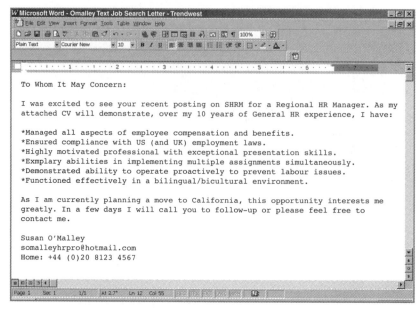

Electronic job search letter for job opening

'Compose' from the tabs along the top of the page. By placing her cursor within the message of the newly created e-mail, Susan can then paste the contents of her custom electronic letter in the message box. Simply choose 'Paste' from the 'edit' pull-down menu (or Cmd+V for Macintosh).

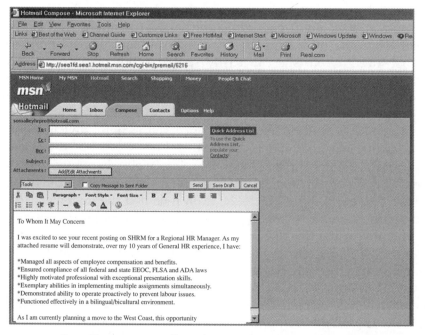

Sending an e-mail to the prospective company

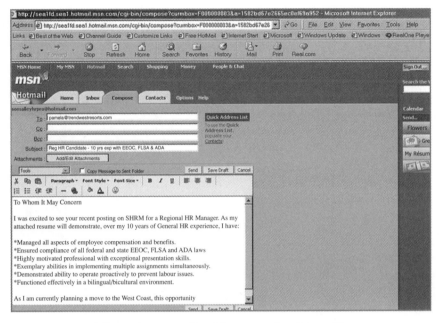

Adding the e-mail address and subject line

With the letter safely pasted in the body of the e-mail, turn your attention to addressing the e-mail to the proper recipient and drafting your subject line. The subject line needs to be factual, professional, yet intriguing. How about 'Your next Reg HR Manager – EEOC, FLSA & ADA exp' or 'Reg HR Candidate – 10 yrs exp w/ EEOC, FLSA & ADA'?

Many people do not realize that the subject line can hold many characters. While a message in your inbox will reveal 60+ characters, an opened or maximized message will show over 150 characters. To be safe, you should keep your subject lines to fewer than 60 characters, including spaces and punctuation. This way, the receiver will see your entire subject at all times.

It's a smart strategy to keep a copy of all correspondence. You can do this by selecting that option from virtually any e-mail program. With Hotmail, there is a small box that can be clicked directly above the message box 'Copy Message to Sent Folder'. This means that a copy of every e-mail you send will be saved in the 'sent' folder. This way, you can always refer back to see what was sent, to whom, and when. In addition, you can always move messages from one folder to another once you have started a communication stream with a particular company.

Finally, we need to talk a little about the CV. Under the subject of the new e-mail Susan created, there is a button for 'Add/Edit Attachments.' In some programs, such as Microsoft Outlook, there is a button that looks like a paper

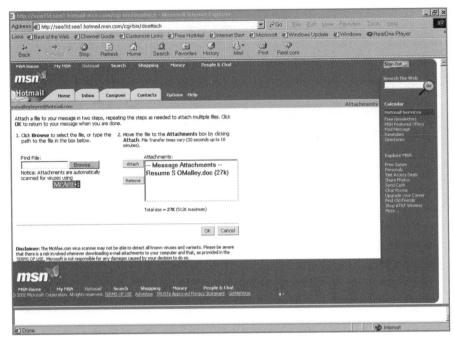

Attaching your CV

clip or a menu choice to insert documents. They all work the same way. Once selected, you will then need to find the document you want to attach. Follow the instructions on the screen. Once you have 'browsed' to locate the file, select 'open'. In Hotmail, once you've browsed and found the file you must then select 'attach'. The name of your file will appear in the attachment box. Continue to follow the instructions and select 'OK'.

Before you send this message, recall two points we addressed earlier when Susan initially found this job posting. First, the employer did not suggest a format in which to send the CV. The most popular is what we have done, but it is not 100 per cent effective if the employer does not have Microsoft Word or cannot, for some reason, open the attachment.

Here's a quick solution. Just as you copy and paste your ASCII letter into the e-mail message box, do the same with your CV. You already have it created – simply go to your 'Text CVs' folder, select the text, copy it, and then return to the e-mail message you just created.

Scroll down through your electronic job search letter. Below your name and contact information insert a few asterisks and then paste the ASCII resume. If the employer has trouble with the attachment, you have sensibly provided a backup solution, which speaks well of your general professional skill sets. Now all that is left to do is to hit the 'send' button.

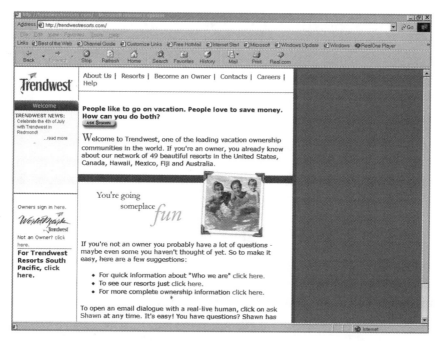

www.trendwestresorts.com

Reaching the Right Person

One challenge with the electronic part of your job search is to reach human eyes. When the job posting does not list a person's name to contact, you may need to do a little sleuthing to find it. From the contact information, we have an e-mail address and a physical address. Often with company e-mail addresses, the Web site of the company is part of the address that comes after the person's username and the '@' symbol. In this case it is safe to assume that if we break up the e-mail address of *jadariav@trendwestresorts.com*, we can probably find the company's home page at *www.trendwestresorts.com*.

Surf the company site and look for a job board, the bios and contacts of company executives and press releases. Your mission is to find another doorway into this company, perhaps another name to whom you can also send your submission with a slightly different job search letter. With a little extra effort, you could establish a direct connection to your next boss and avoid the corporate CV database altogether. You might also gather other useful information about the company that will help you stand out at the interview.

Electronic Signatures and 'Fake' Real Stationery

Although not terribly difficult, I group these tools with Web and HTML CVs – if you are in a creative or Web design profession, then you probably need them to show your technical and creative expertise. The rest of us can make better use of our time. However, if you are determined to use these tools, or if the majority of professionals you know use electronic signatures or stationery, then go ahead and try it.

While most of the free e-mail programs will not support these fancy features, they are available in both Microsoft Outlook and Outlook Express. By going to your e-mail program and choosing the 'Tools' menu button and then selecting 'Options', you will find a box full of many options to customize your e-mail. Under 'Options', if you select 'Mail Format', you will find both the stationery and signature capabilities.

Although I advise against the use of e-mail stationery or any unusual fonts, I will propose a middle ground on the signature – use the many fonts available in your word processing program. When you receive an e-mail that contains what appears to be a real signature, someone has actually signed, scanned and digitized their signature, imbedding it into the body of the message. However, you should never use your real signature – with a minimum of technical expertise, anyone could copy it and electronic signatures can have the same legal validity as a written signature. Don't risk your online security.

Do not think for a moment that you see my signature in the following message. My handwriting has never been that legible, nor would I compromise my identity in this way. It is really just a font. Much less effort than scanning in your true signature and risking your credit line.

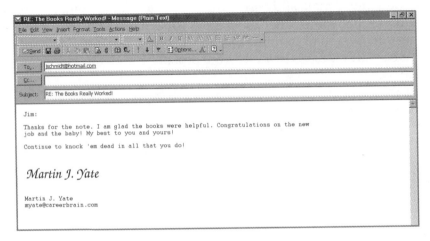

E-mail with fake signature

Accuracy Is Essential

Maybe your family doesn't mind the jokes with misspelt words. Perhaps your colleagues forgive typos, understanding that you are busy. But this is your job hunt, and you need to put your best professional foot forward. Under 'Options' choose 'Spelling', as shown below.

Now this is a truly useful little tool. Here you can set your e-mail to check spelling before each and every message is sent. Set this feature to always check before sending, but never forget that automatic spellchecking is not perfect.

Before you send any online communication, take a deep breath and remember to proof your CVs, job search letters and any other career communications. Practice using your e-mail and send electronic letters and CV attachments to yourself, friends, family members and colleagues. Have friends print your practice e-mail messages and CVs – make sure that what you think you are sending is actually received.

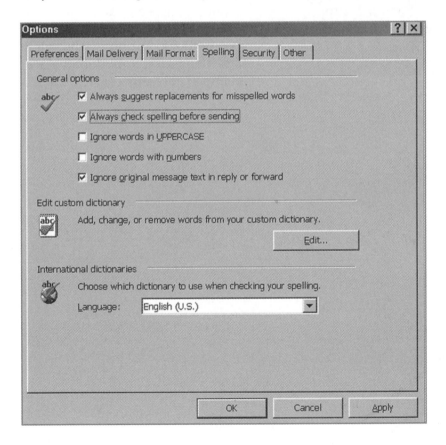

Spell-checking options

8

Sample Letters

Here's the real meat of the book the sample letters you can use as models for your own.

Now we come to the letters. Apart from the sender's name and address (the personal stationery aspect), all letters adhere to Houghton Mifflin's *Best Writer's Guide* specifications. To those who might notice these things, it is important that we present an impeccable attention to detail.

E-mail Response to Online Job Posting
(Technical Sales Representative)

Dear Ms _____,

Please accept this letter as application for the Technical Sales Representative position currently available with your company, as listed on Monster.com. My confidential CV is attached for your review and consideration, and I believe you will find me well qualified.

Detailed on my CV you will find a solid background in Sales and Marketing, with over two years in technical sales. In this capacity, I have developed an expertise in new and key account acquisition, new territory development and management, contract negotiation, and customer service. I am confident that my experience in these areas will prove to be an asset to ABC Ltd.

In addition, I am familiar with blueprints, part number breakdowns, and the bidding process of our major accounts, which include _____, _____, _____ and _____ plc. I have doubled my sales from £30,000/month to £60,000/month in just two years, and I am known for effectively identifying and resolving problems before they affect related areas, personnel or customers.

I would welcome the opportunity to discuss with you how I might make similar contributions to the success of ABC Ltd. I look forward to hearing from you to schedule a personal interview at a time convenient to you.

Sincere regards,

Jane Swift
020 8123 4567
jane@anyaddress.co.uk

E-mail Response to Online Job Posting (Teacher)

Dear Ms _____,

I noted with interest your 13 June, 2003 job posting on CareerCity.com for a Year 2 Teacher for a leave replacement (9/03–12/03). As a qualified teacher with experience teaching this level and first-hand knowledge of children through extensive volunteer activities, I believe that I am an excellent candidate for this position.

I understand that you need someone who is self-directed and who possesses the necessary qualities for managing another teacher's class – flexibility, good humour, rapport with parents, familiarity with the school culture, and the ability to go beyond the lesson plans in accordance with meeting the current needs. At this point, I welcome the challenge of making a positive impact on the minds of primary school-aged children. I am committed to achieving this goal through ongoing professional development to learn the latest effective teaching methods.

I have attached my CV to provide more information on my strengths and career achievements. I am also open to other opportunities in the school. If after reviewing my material you believe that there is a match, please call me. Thank you for your consideration.

Sincere regards,

Jane Swift
020 8123 4567
jane@anyaddress.co.uk

E-mail Response to Online Job Posting
(Investment Banker)

Dear Mr _____,

In response to your job posting for a _____ on your company's Web site, I have attached my CV for your consideration.

My experience as an administrative investment banker and assistant to a Director is, I believe, readily adaptable to your needs. I have spent five years in a position best described as 'doing whatever needs to be done' and have capitalized on my ability to undertake a large and widely varied array of projects, learn quickly, find effective solutions to problems, and maintain a sense of humour throughout.

My years as a line and administrative professional have also provided me with an unusual sensitivity to the needs of senior professionals. I have substantial computer experience and am fully computer literate. I have been told my verbal and written communication skills are exceptional.

I believe your firm would provide a working atmosphere to which I would be well suited, as well as one where my diverse experience would be valuable.

My salary requirements are reasonable and negotiable based on the responsibilities and opportunities presented.

Sincerely,

Jane Swift
020 8123 4567
jane@anyaddress.co.uk

E-mail Response to Online Job Posting
(Legal Administrator)

Dear Ms _____,

I am responding to your job posting on Hotjobs.com for a legal administrator of a law firm. I wrote to you on [date] about law administrator positions in the _____ area. I have attached another CV of my educational background and employment history. I am very interested in this position.

I have been a legal administrator for two law firms during the past six years. In addition, I have been a law firm consultant for over a year. Besides my law firm experience, I have been a medical administrator for over 10 years. I believe that all of this experience will enable me to manage the law firm for this position very successfully. I possess the management, marketing, computer, accounting/budgeting, financial planning, personnel, and people-oriented skills that would have a very positive impact on this law firm.

I will be in the _____ area later in the month, so I hope, we can meet at that time to discuss this position. I look forward to hearing from you, Ms _____, concerning this position. Thank you for your time and consideration.

Very truly yours,

Jane Swift
020 8123 4567
jane@anyaddress.co.uk

E-mail Response to Online Job Posting
(Human Resources)

Dear _____,

Attached is my CV containing pertinent information regarding my qualifications. I am confident that my knowledge and abilities could be used to enhance your Human Resources Department.

The following experience, skills and strengths are key elements that qualify me for consideration:

- Extensive background in HR, administrative support and office management functions.
- Highly motivated professional with exceptional people skills.
- Proven skills in organizing, prioritizing and managing with maximum efficiency.
- Exemplary abilities in implementing multiple assignments simultaneously.
- Demonstrated ability to identify and resolve problems.
- Flexible and adapt well to changing organizational needs.
- Possess excellent communication skills and enjoy interacting as a team member.
- Ability to develop and implement new procedures.
- Function effectively in a bilingual / bicultural environment.

I would enjoy meeting you to discuss your company's plans and how I can contribute to its ongoing success. In a few days I will ring you to follow-up or please feel free to contact me.

Sincerely,

Jane Swift
020 8123 4567
jane@anyaddress.co.uk

E-mail Response to Online Job Posting (Manufacturing)

Dear Sir/Madam,

Please accept the attached CV in application for a position with your company that will make use of my extensive background in material handling, shipping, receiving and warehousing. Throughout my career I have demonstrated my loyalty, commitment to excellence and solid work ethic. I am confident that I will make an immediate and long-term contribution to your company.

For the past 26 years, I have been successfully working in manufacturing and warehouse settings. I am a hard working employee who always looks for ways to improve productivity, efficiency and accuracy. In past positions, I have identified ways to reduce down time and waste, as well as methods to increase production.

I am dedicated to the principles of quality, continuous improvement and customer satisfaction. My supervisor has noted my record of 'excellent attendance and dependability' and praised me as 'reliable and highly motivated'.

I would like to meet you to discuss my qualifications. Please call me at the following phone number, or leave a message, to arrange an interview. Thank you for your consideration.

Sincerely,

James Swift
020 8123 4567
james@anyaddress.co.uk

E-mail Response to Online Job Posting
(Production Supervisor)

Dear Ms _____,

In response to the job posting on your company's Web site, please consider my CV in your search for a Production Supervisor.

With a hi-tech background in Blue Chip companies, I feel well qualified for the position you described. I am presently responsible for the coordination of production in three assembly and test areas which employ 35 personnel. Maintaining control of work of this magnitude and complexity requires my ability to function independently, and a willingness to make decisions quickly and effectively.

I am accustomed to a fast-paced environment where deadlines are a priority and handling multiple jobs simultaneously is the norm. I enjoy a challenge and work hard to attain my goals. Constant negotiations with all levels of management and employees have strengthened my interpersonal skills. I would like very much to discuss with you how I could contribute to your organization.

I am seeking an opportunity to excel in a more dynamic company and am looking forward to relocating to the _____ area.

Please contact me at your earliest convenience so that I may share with you my background and enthusiasm for the job. Thank you for your time and consideration.

Sincerely,

James Swift
020 8123 4567
james@anyaddress.co.uk

E-mail Response to Online Job Posting
(Applications Support Specialist)

Dear Ms _____,

As a proficient computer professional with four years of experience in software applications design, development, testing and maintenance for clients, I am particularly qualified for the Applications Support Specialist position at your company.

Currently an Applications Consultant with a company specializing in healthcare software applications, I offer a solid background in system applications, development, customer support and project management.

In my present role, I manage the implementation of our clients' nursing applications for client/server and other platforms. Client evaluation, product demonstrations, design/development of application solutions, support throughout the implementation cycle, on-site client training in system customization and use, as well as system audits are among my primary responsibilities. With solid project planning, coordinating and management skills, I have a successful track record in delivering results within deadline.

In addition, my position involves strong troubleshooting, research and writing/updating technical documentation for applications. I test, troubleshoot and maintain software applications on a daily basis, working closely with our QA group. An excellent problem solver, I am able to get to the root of an issue quickly and design a solution. In providing technical support, one of my strengths is to treat each customer as a key account that deserves outstanding service and response.

As part of a team-oriented environment, I also mentor new employees, providing ongoing coaching and training to assist them in professional development. I plan to relocate back to the Manchester area and would welcome the opportunity to join your team. I am confident that I possess the necessary technical knowledge and skills to add value to your company. May we meet to discuss your needs further?

Sincerely,

James Swift
020 8123 4567
james@anyaddress.co.uk

E-mail Response to Online Job Posting
(Production Manager)

Dear Mr _____,

I am interested in employment as a production manager with your firm. I know that my education and experience have prepared me for the position you have available.

For the past 10 years I have worked as a manager in manufacturing facilities. My company's annual evaluations of me have cited my ability to get the job done 'on time and under budget', as well as the high employee morale in my department. I also have extensive hands-on experience as a machinist. Details of my education and experience are in the enclosed CV.

I know I can make a significant contribution to your company. May I come in, at a time convenient to you, so we can discuss my qualifications more fully?

Sincerely,

James Swift
020 8123 4567
james@anyaddress.co.uk

Response to Newspaper Advertisement
(Assessment Coordinator)

18 Park Street, London X1 0BB   **JANE SWIFT**
020 8123 4567
jane@anyaddress.co.uk

2 PAGES VIA FAX   [Date]
DEPT HD 020 7123 4567

Your advertisement in the *The Times*, on 9 June, 2000, for an **Assessment Coordinator** seems
to perfectly match my background and experience. As the International Brand Coordinator for
ABC, I coordinated meetings, prepared presentations and materials, organized a major off-site
conference, and supervised an assistant. I believe that I am an excellent candidate for this
position as I have illustrated below:

YOUR REQUIREMENTS	MY QUALIFICATIONS
A highly motivated, diplomatic, flexible, quality-driven professional	Successfully managed project teams involving different business units. The defined end results were achieved on every project.
Exceptional organizational skills and attention to detail	Planned the development and launch of the ABC Heritage Edition bottle series. My former manager enjoyed leaving the 'details' and follow-through to me. Undertook project management training.
College degree and minimum 3 years relevant business experience	BA from London University (1994). 5+ years business experience in productive, professional environments.
Computer literacy	Extensive knowledge of Windows & Macintosh applications.

I'm interested in this position because it fits well with my new career focus in the human
resources field. Currently, I am enrolled on an adult career planning and development
certificate programme and working at XYZ.

I have enclosed my CV to provide more information on my strengths and career
achievements. If after reviewing my material you believe that there is a match, please ring me.
Thank you for your consideration.

Yours faithfully,

Jane Swift

Jane Swift

enclosure

Response to Newspaper Advertisement
(Office Administrator)

JANE SWIFT
18 Park Street, London X1 0BB
020 8123 4567   jane@anyaddress.co.uk

[Date]

Philip _____
[title]
ABC Ltd
Industry Square
London X2 2EF

Dear Ms _____,

Your notice for an **Office Administrator** caught my attention because my background appears to parallel your needs. Please refer to the enclosed CV for a summary of my qualifications. I am sure you have been flooded with hundreds of qualified applicants; please allow me to explain why you would want to call me first.

    I am very **self-sufficient** and able to **work independently with little supervision**. With little formal training, I have taken the initiative to learn about and remain current with my company's products, processes and expectations. I am looked at as **an information resource** and enjoy sharing my knowledge with others. I also enjoy **managing projects** and **planning meetings**, **trips and special events**.

    I am always looking for ways to **streamline processes** and become more efficient. I have **developed systems and processes** using available software to automate production reporting, notify customers of changes, and inform the field staff of corporate changes or initiatives. When supervising clerical staff, I always try to **plan ahead** to make the best use of their time.

    I work well with executives, sales representatives, customers, vendors and co-workers, and demonstrate strong interpersonal communication skills and good judgement. I always try to listen closely and understand what others need. Then, I look for ways to help solve the problem. I have particularly found that listening, without interrupting, can diffuse a tense situation and allow the issue to be resolved more quickly with a positive outcome.

    I am confident that I can deliver similar results for ABC Ltd. I would appreciate the opportunity to speak to you to schedule an appointment and provide you with more information. Thank you for your time and consideration; I look forward to speaking to you soon.

Sincerely,

Jane Swift

Jane Swift

enclosure

Response to Newspaper Advertisement
(Library Director)

JANE SWIFT
18 Park Street, London X1 0BB   ●   020 8123 4567 jane@anyaddress.co.uk

[Date]

Philip _____
[title]
Anytown Public Library
Industry Square
London X2 2EF

Dear Mr _____,

   Your recent advertisement for a Library Director to lead the Anytown Public Library Service has captured my interest. As a library professional with 20-plus years' experience, I have expertise directly relevant to this leadership role.

   Among the experiences that I can bring to this opportunity are the following:

- *Serving as Director of a dynamic, multi-branch library in North Lincolnshire. The County Library had an annual circulation of 725,000 items, 78 employees, and a £1.9 million budget. In this role, I developed and administered the budget, including presenting the budget proposal to the County Council.*
- *Maintaining a strong rapport with the County Council. I actively participated on numerous County Library System committees and advisory groups.*
- *Heading the Interlibrary Loan department of the Public Library Service, which provided services regionally to over 124 individual libraries in the area. In addition to directly supervising staff, I participated on regional and national committees addressing issues related to interlibrary loan.*
- *Managing capital projects and spearheading information technology initiatives, which encompassed discussions of how best to incorporate the newest innovations into library settings.*

   The size and character of the North Lincolnshire community and the libraries that serve it are similar to the area your library serves, and I'm sure they face many of the same challenges. I believe that my 20-plus year career has exposed me to virtually every facet of library management and prepared me for a significant leadership role, such as the Directorship of the Anytown Public Library Service. I am convinced that my knowledge and expertise would allow me to substantially contribute to furthering the library's mission. I look forward to discussing my candidacy with you in detail at a mutually convenient time.
   Since my current employer is unaware of my job search, I trust that this correspondence will be held in strict confidence.

Sincerely,

Jane Swift

Jane Swift

enclosure

Response to Newspaper Advertisement
(Marketing Manager)

James Swift
18 Park Street, London X1 0BB
020 8123 4567   james@anyaddress.co.uk

[Date]

Emily _____
[Title]
ABC Ltd
Industry Square
London X2 2EF

Dear Ms _____,

Your recent advertisement for a New Products Marketing Manager in the 31 May *Sunday Times* really captured my attention, as your requirements are a *custom-fit* to my experience and interests. For the past six years I have pursued an increasingly successful career in marketing management. My management and marketing *skills* enabled me to achieve extremely high performance levels.

I am confident that my comprehensive management experience would serve as an asset to your organization. My record is one of increased responsibility, variety in job assignments, and solid accomplishments. The enclosed CV will provide you with a brief outline of my experience and accomplishments. Please allow me to highlight my skills as they relate to your stated requirements:

YOUR REQUIREMENTS	MY QUALIFICATIONS
Drive and manage the marketing of new product development projects and product launch	*Launched* 900 MHz communication product *driving sales growth from £1M to £28M*. *Increased volume* from 10k units (product predecessor) to over 500k units sold in the first year.
Solicit and evaluate new project ideas	Conducted face-to-face meetings with retail buyers, at the national level, to obtain market feedback. *Spearheaded development* of multi-faceted product tailored to specific needs and produced customized marketing plan.
Perform market/competitive analysis, conduct market research and concept testing	*Demonstrated success in analysing marketplace* to develop matrix that demonstrates superiority of product line.
Ability to manage independent projects/work on new product development	Proven ability to *identify trends* by category using product profiles. Conduct focus groups to enhance ease of use, determine feature mix, and identify colours and optimal packaging to *achieve significant product improvement/new product*.

James Swift
page 2 of 2

▪ MBA degree preferred   ▪ Hold MBA in ***Marketing Management*** from
                                              London University.

I am accustomed to a *fast-paced* environment where deadlines are a priority and handling
multiple jobs simultaneously is the norm. Continual interaction with clients, in addition to all
levels of management and operations, have strengthened my interpersonal and negotiation
skills. I approach my work with a strong sense of urgency, working well under pressure and
change. I look forward to meeting you personally so that we may discuss in greater detail how
my expertise would best meet the needs of your organization. In the interim, thank you for
your consideration, attention and forthcoming response.

Best regards,

James Swift

James Swift

enclosure

Response to Newspaper Advertisement
(Legal Secretary)

JANE SWIFT
18 Park Street, London X1 0BB
020 8123 4567   jane@address.co.uk

[Date]

Emily _____
[Title]
General Council of the Bar
Industry Square
London X2 2EF

RE: GENERAL COUNCIL OF THE BAR, LEGAL SECRETARY

Dear Mr Davis,
   It is with continued interest and enthusiasm that I respond to your advertisement for Legal Secretary to the General Council of the Bar. I believe that my education and experience combine to create a perfect match for the position, and would appreciate careful consideration of my credentials as presented below and within my CV, enclosed.
   It has long been my dream to pursue a career in the legal arena, and my goal to associate with the top professionals in the field. Where better to continue my professional development than within the heart of the organization as a provider of administrative support to members of the Bar itself!
   Although a relative newcomer to the field, I have earned my HNC in Legal Studies and Paralegal Certificate. With more than two years of experience after qualifying, providing administrative and clerical support in private practice, I am confident that I possess the expertise and dedication that will make an immediate and significant contribution to the efficiency and organization of the Council.
   If you are looking for a legal support professional who is committed to the highest standards of performance, relates well to others, is self-directing and highly motivated, and is looking for a long-term employment relationship, please contact me to arrange an interview. I will make myself available at your earliest convenience.
   Thank you for your consideration; I look forward to the opportunity to speak to you soon.

Sincerely yours,

Jane Swift

Jane Swift

enclosure (CV and Professional References)

Response to Newspaper Advertisement
(Accounting Manager)

James Swift
18 Park Street, London X1 0BB
020 8123 4567　james@anyaddress.co.uk

[Date]

Phillip _____
[Title]
ABC Ltd
Industry Square
London X2 2EF

Dear Mr _____,

Re: File No. 213

I have nine years of accounting experience and am responding to your recent advertisement for an Accounting Manager. Please allow me to highlight my skills as they relate to your stated requirements:

Your Requirements	My Experience
A recognized accounting qualification plus several years of practical accounting experience.	Obtained CIMA membership and have over four years' practical experience as an Accounting Manager.
Excellent people skills and demonstrated ability to motivate staff.	Effectively managed a staff of 24 including two supervisors.
Strong administrative and analytical skills.	Assisted in the development of a base reference library with Microsoft Excel for 400 clients.
Good oral and written communication skills.	Trained four new supervisors via daily coaching sessions, communication meetings and technical skill sessions.

I believe this background provides the management skills you require for this position. I would welcome the opportunity for a personal interview to further discuss my qualifications.

Yours truly,

James Swift

James Swift

enclosure

Response to Newspaper Advertisement
(International Sales Manager)

Jane Swift
18 Park Street, London X1 0BB
020 8123 4567   jane@anyaddress.co.uk

[Date]

Phillip _____
[Title]
ABC Ltd
Industry Square
London X2 2EF

Dear Mr _____,

Re: International Sales Manager, *Globe & Mail*, — September, 20 —

I was recently speaking with Mr _____ from your firm and he strongly recommended that I send you a copy of my CV. Knowing the requirements for the position, he felt that I would be an ideal candidate. For more than eleven years I have been involved in international sales management, with seven years directly in the aerospace industry. My qualifications for the position include:

- establishing sales offices in France, Germany and Italy;
- recruiting and managing a group of 24 international sales representatives;
- providing training programmes for all of the international staff, which included full briefing on our own products as well as competitor lines;
- obtaining 42%, 33% and 31% of the French, German and Italian markets, respectively, dealing with all local engine and airframe manufacturers; and
- generating more than £32 million in sales with excellent margins.

My Bachelor of Science degree in Electrical Engineering was obtained from the University of _____ and my languages include French, German and Italian.

I feel confident that an interview would demonstrate that my expertise in setting up representative organizations and training and managing an international sales department would be an excellent addition to your growing aerospace corporation.

I look forward to meeting with you, Mr _____, and will ring you to follow up on this letter the week of [date] _____.

Yours truly,

Jane Swift

Jane Swift

enclosure

Response to Newspaper Advertisement
(Executive Assistant)

JAMES SWIFT
18 Park Street ● London X1 0BB
020 8123 4567   james@anyaddress.co.uk

[Date]

Box 9412
London X2 2EF

Dear _____,

I was very pleased to learn of the need for an Executive Assistant in your company from your recent advertisement in _____. I believe the qualities you seek are well matched by my track record:

Your Needs	My Qualifications
Independent Self-Starter	▪ Served as company liaison between sales representatives, controlling commissions and products.
	▪ Controlled cash flow, budget planning and bank reconciliation for three companies.
	▪ Assisted in the promotion of a restaurant within a private placement sales effort, creating sales materials and communicating with investors.
Computer Experience	▪ Used Lotus in preparing financial spreadsheet for private placement memoranda and Macintosh to design brochures and flyers.
	▪ Have vast experience with both computer programming and the current software packages.
Compatible Background	▪ Spent 5 years overseas and speak French.
	▪ Served as an executive assistant to four corporate heads.

A CV is enclosed that covers my experience and qualifications in greater detail. I would appreciate the opportunity to discuss my credentials in a personal interview.

Sincerely,

James Swift

James Swift

enclosure

Power Phrases

Consider using adaptations of these key phrases in your responses to newspaper advertisements.

I believe that I am particularly well qualified for your position and would like to have the opportunity to meet you to explore how I may be of value to your organization.

Your advertisement 5188 in the 25th March edition of The _____ has piqued my interest. This position has strong appeal to me.

I am confident that with my abilities I can make an immediate and valuable contribution to _____.

I would be pleased if you contacted me for an interview.

I was recently speaking with Mr _____ from your firm and he strongly recommended that I send you a copy of my CV. Knowing the requirements for the position, he felt that I would be an ideal candidate.

I've had both large and small company experience and it is my preference to work in a smaller operation where goals are measurable, results are noticeable and contributions really make a difference!

I feel confident that an interview would demonstrate that my expertise in setting up representative organizations, and training and managing an international sales department, would be an excellent addition to your growing _____ company.

I look forward to meeting you, Mr _____, and will give you a ring to follow up on this letter the week of —th September.

The opportunity to work with your client is appealing to me, and I would appreciate an opportunity to discuss the position further. I look forward to hearing from you soon.

I believe this background provides the management skills you require for this position. I would welcome the opportunity for a personal interview to further discuss my qualifications.

In response to your advertisement, please consider my CV in your search for a Sales Service Coordinator.

I look forward to hearing from you in the near future to schedule an interview at a time convenient to you, during which I hope to learn more about your company's plans and goals and how I might contribute to the success of its service team.

I am accustomed to a fast-paced environment where deadlines are a priority and handling multiple jobs simultaneously is the norm. I enjoy a challenge and work hard to attain my goals. Constant negotiations with all levels of management and employees have strengthened my interpersonal skills. I would like very much to discuss with you how I could contribute to your organization.

I am seeking an opportunity to excel in a dynamic company and am looking forward to relocating to _____.

Please contact me at your earliest convenience so that I may share with you my background and enthusiasm for the job.

Your advertisement captured my attention.

My personal goal is simple: I wish to be a part of an organization that wants to excel in both _____ and _____. I believe that if I had the opportunity of an interview with you it would be apparent that my skills are far-reaching.

Although I'm far more interested in a fine company and an intriguing challenge than merely in money, you should know that in recent years my compensation has been in the range of £30,000 to £40,000.

May we set up a time to talk?

What you need and what I can do sound like a match!

_Please find enclosed a copy of my CV for your review. I believe the combination of my _____ education and my business experience offers me the unique opportunity to make a positive contribution to your firm._

As you will note in my CV, I have not only 'grown up' in and with the Operations and Warehousing area of a major (clothing) (consumer products) company, I have also established my expertise and my value to a discriminating and brilliant employer who depended upon me – on a daily basis – to represent and protect his interests and contribute significantly to his profitability.... I am seeking an opportunity to replicate this situation and again use my considerable abilities to dedicate myself to the profitability of my employer.

_I am available to meet you to discuss my qualifications at a time convenient to you. I can be reached at _____. I would like to thank you in advance for your time and any consideration you may give me. I look forward to hearing from you._

_Having been born and raised in the _____ area and wishing to return to this area to work as a _____, I have been researching _____ firms that offer the type of experience for which my education and work experience would be of mutual benefit. Highlights of my attached CV include: _____._

_Please consider my qualifications for the position of _____ which you advertised._

As you will note on the enclosed CV, the breadth of my expertise covers a wide area of responsibilities, thereby providing me with insights into the total operation.

_Recently, I saw an advertisement in the _____ for a position as a Technical Trainer. My candidacy for this position is advanced by my experience in three areas: training, support and a technological background._

I thrive on challenge and feel that my skills and experience are easily transferable.

I would appreciate an opportunity to discuss my abilities in more depth, and am available for an interview at your earliest convenience.

Is the ideal candidate for the position of _____ highly motivated, professional and knowledgeable in all functions concerning _____? Well, you may be interested to know that a person possessing these qualities, and much more, is responding to your advertisement in the _____ for this position.

I very much enjoy working in a team environment and the rewards associated with group contribution.

The skills you require seem to match my professional strengths.

I have a strong background in telemarketing small and medium-size businesses in the _____ district and outlying areas.

I look forward to hearing from you soon to set up an appointment at a time convenient to you. Please feel free to ring me at my office on _____ or leave a message at my home number, _____.

As a recent MBA graduate, my professional job experience is necessarily limited. However, I believe that you will find, and previous employers will verify, that I exhibit intelligence, common sense, initiative, maturity and stability, and I am eager to make a positive contribution to your organization.

I read with a great deal of interest your advertisement in the 20 October _____, issue of _____.

Please allow me to highlight some of my achievements which relate to your requirements: _____.

I would greatly appreciate the opportunity to discuss this position in a personal interview. I may be contacted at _____ to arrange a meeting.

I would appreciate an opportunity to meet you. At present I am working as a temp but am available to meet you whenever would be convenient for you. I look forward to meeting you.

Thank you for taking the time recently to respond to my questions concerning a _____ position with _____.

I will be in your area on Friday —th December, and will call you early next week to see if we might schedule a meeting at that time.

_This experience has provided me with a keen appreciation of the general practice of _____ ._

A salary of £30,000 would be acceptable; however, my main concern is to find employment where there is potential for growth.

'Cold' E-mail – To a Potential Employer
(Summer Placement)

Dear Mr _____,

If you are seeking a student with a strong desire to apply current knowledge, strong work ethics and an ability to find success in any situation, then look no further. Please accept this letter and attached CV as an expression of interest in pursuing a work experience position with your organization.

As my CV indicates, I have advanced education, hands-on training and real-life experience in various fields of the fashion and entertainment industry and am currently pursuing completion of my HND in visual merchandising. For me, a career in fashion is not a sudden decision or a whim; it is a career goal I have been working towards for several years. I am constantly seeking avenues of education and experience that will help me in achieving my goals. As a means to achieving those goals, I am very interested in working for your organization and gaining practical experience and additional knowledge in the real world.

In return for the opportunity to gain the experience and knowledge I seek, I offer you a highly motivated, enthusiastic and proactive team member who will go above and beyond in the pursuit of any task given. I am willing and able to travel and reside in any location during my work experience and can make myself available for interviews whenever is convenient for you.

I welcome any opportunity to elaborate on how I could make a meaningful contribution to your organization. Thank you for your consideration. I look forward to speaking to you soon.

Sincerely,

Jane Swift
020 8123 4567
jane@anyaddress.co.uk

'Cold' E-mail – To a Potential Employer
(Financial Analyst)

Dear Ms _____,

Like many other recent graduates, I am searching for an opportunity to use my professional skills while contributing to a company's growth and success. Unlike some others, however, I don't believe that a new **Master's degree in Finance** is enough of a qualification in today's competitive marketplace.

Therefore, I have worked hard to supplement my education with hands-on experience in the financial arena, giving me a broad range of skills necessary to begin a career as a **Financial Analyst**. Through my employment and academic studies, I have developed the qualifications that would make me an asset to your company:

- **Financial services:** Demonstrated initiative in identifying and securing valuable professional experience with some of the top financial companies in the country, which provided me with valuable hands-on experience and the opportunity to contribute immediately.

- **Research, analytical and problem-solving strengths:** A flexible thinker, I chose an educational programme that required careful analysis and examination of factors with rigorous insistence on logic. I have the ability to research, assess and synthesize information, as well as look at problems from many different perspectives to arrive at creative solutions.

- **Communication:** Written reports and research papers as well as presentations were an ongoing part of my university coursework as well as my employment experiences.

If you foresee the need for a capable professional with the ability, education, experience and attitude to make a difference to your organization, then we should meet to discuss your needs and how I may contribute. Thank you for your consideration.

Very truly yours,

James Swift
020 8123 4567
james@anyaddress.co.uk

'Cold' E-mail – To a Potential Employer (Administration)

Dear Mr _____,

Are you looking for a seasoned administrator with diversified experience in human resources management, financial services management, project leadership and operational audits? I have 17 years of human resources experience with extensive knowledge in staffing, strategic planning, compensation and benefits administration, research and policy development, employee relations and employee relocation.

I am seeking a position in the human resources area; however, I am interested in other administrative management opportunities that require my abilities.

I have attached my CV and I look forward to hearing from you to discuss my qualifications further.

Sincerely,

Jane Swift
020 8123 4567
jane@anyaddress.co.uk

'Cold' E-mail – To a Potential Employer
(Banking)

Dear Mr _____,

Please include my name in your job search database. As requested, I have attached a copy of my current CV.

Banking today is definitely a sales environment. While my marketing skills will always be useful, my interests lead me now to seek a more distinct financial management position such as Controller, Treasurer or Head of Finance.

Since my CIMA Part III will be completed in January 20—, my search may be somewhat premature, but my transcript and results, combined with my practical experience, should offset my temporary lack of an accounting qualification. I would therefore like you to consider me immediately. As an Account Manager, I saw many different industries, and so would not feel constrained to any one sector.

Including a mortgage loan benefit, I am currently earning £3,000 per month plus a car allowance. This should provide you with an indication of my present job level. Your suggestions or comments would be appreciated. I am available for interviews, and can be reached at 020 8123 4567. Thank you.

Yours truly,

James Swift

james@anyaddress.co.uk

'Cold' E-mail – To a Potential Employer
(Software Development)

Dear Mr _____,

ABC Ltd caught my attention recently as I began a search for a new employer in the London area. ABC Ltd is well known in the software industry for quality products and excellent customer service; it also maintains a strong reputation as a great employer. Your organization has created an environment in which people can excel, which is why I am writing to you today.

I am very interested in joining your software development team. I am confident that my background and experience will meet your future needs. My current position is Application Developer for XYZ. I enjoy it very much as it has provided me with extensive hands-on training in Visual Basic and other languages. However, I am ready to get more into the actual software writing, as well as return to the London area. I possess a bachelor's degree in Computer Science as well as training in a variety of programming languages. I am also a fast learner, as demonstrated by my learning Visual Basic quickly after joining XYZ. In addition, I plan to pursue my Master's degree and have begun the application process.

I would appreciate the opportunity to meet you to discuss your goals and how I can help you meet them. I will ring you soon to arrange a meeting that is convenient for you. In the meantime, please feel free to ring me for further information on my background and experience.

Thank you for your consideration and reply. I look forward to meeting you in the near future.

Yours truly,

Jane Swift
020 8123 4567
jane@anyaddress.co.uk

'Cold' E-mail – To a Potential Employer
(Retail Administration)

Dear Mr _____,

After 15 years in the retail administration field, I am seeking a new position and have attached my CV for your consideration.

You will notice one common thread throughout my career – I am an administrator and a problem solver. These talents have been applied successfully in office management, field operations, purchasing, communications, telephone skills, and organizing and structuring of various departments. These assignments have required close coordination with Senior Management. This diversity of accomplishments enables me to relate to other areas of business.

I am self-motivated and can work independently to get the job done efficiently in the least possible time.

I will be ringing you on Friday – th August to be sure you received my CV and answer any questions you might have.

Very truly yours,

James Swift
020 8123 4567
james@anyaddress.co.uk

'Cold' E-mail – To a Potential Employer
(Corporate Communications)

Dear Ms _____,

Perhaps you are seeking an addition to your communications team. A new person can provide innovative approaches to the challenges and opportunities of integrated corporate communications. You will discover from the attached CV that I have a results-oriented background in several key areas.

Although my career has been centred on well-established public relations agencies, I prefer to continue professionally on the client side. In fact, in a couple of instances (both here and overseas), I worked on-site within the client organization.

I want to concentrate my diverse talents in the service of one company's communications efforts. I currently would consider opportunities in the £40–£50K range.

Feel free to ring me to discuss any details.

Yours sincerely,

Jane Swift
020 8123 4567
jane@anyaddress.co.uk

'Cold' E-mail – To a Potential Employer
(Process Engineer)

Dear Mr _____,

Please accept this letter as an application for the Process Engineer position currently available with your company. My confidential CV is attached for your review and consideration.

My experience has afforded me exposure to numerous facets of process engineering, including troubleshooting, problem solving, tooling set-up, performance improvement projects and quality assurance. I am confident that my expertise in these areas will prove to be an asset to ABC Ltd's manufacturing operations.

My current salary requirement would be in the mid-to high-20ks, with specifics flexible, negotiable and dependent upon such factors as benefit structure, responsibility and advancement opportunity.

I look forward to hearing from you in the near future to schedule an interview at a time of your convenience, during which I hope to learn more about your company, its plans and goals, and how I might contribute to its continued success.

Sincerely,

James Swift
020 8123 4567
james@anyaddress.co.uk

'Cold' E-mail – To a Potential Employer
(Work Experience)

Dear Ms _____,

I am interested in being considered for a work experience position. I am currently in my second year at the University of London reading International Studies and Political Science with a concentration on Latin America.

My work experience has increased my knowledge of International Relations and enabled me to make use of my education in a professional environment. I am very serious about my International Relations education and future career and am eager to learn as much as possible. I am interested in working for your organization to gain practical experience and additional knowledge pertaining to my field of study.

My professional and academic background, along with my sincere interest in helping others, has enhanced my sensitivity to a diverse range of cultures. As a highly motivated professional, I enjoy the challenge of complex, demanding assignments. My well-developed writing and communication skills are assets to an office environment.

I welcome the opportunity to elaborate on how I could make a substantial contribution to your organization. I look forward to talking to you soon. Thank you.

Sincerely,

Jane Swift
020 8123 4567
jane@anyaddress.co.uk

'Cold' Job Search Letter – To a Potential Employer (Director)

James Swift
18 Park Street ● London X1 0BB
020 8123 4567   james@anyaddress.co.uk

[Date]

Emily_____
[Title]
ABC Ltd
Industry Square
London X2 2EF

Dear Ms _____,

As a Chief Financial Officer, I have built a reputation for my strong ability to provide decisive leadership. For the past few years, my career as a senior-level executive has provided me with opportunities to promote high-level strategic business and financial planning goals for worldwide multi-million pound corporations. My ability to identify challenges and capitalize upon opportunities to expand revenue growth, reduce operating costs and improve overall productivity has been one of my strongest assets to my employers.

My strengths in financial and accounting management as well as my thorough understanding of finance operations have vastly contributed to my career and success as a leader. I maintain self-confidence, credibility and stature to make things happen with colleagues inside and outside the company. Just as significant are my abilities to develop rapport among co-workers and management, build effective teams and promote team effort.

My objective is to secure a position as a CFO or Director and to pursue new opportunities with an organization providing new and exciting challenges. Having a complete picture of my expertise and experience is very important. As you will note in my CV, I have made significant contributions to my employers and take my job very seriously.

I appreciate your time and consideration and will be in contact next week to see if we are able to arrange a meeting date for an interview. I look forward to speaking to you soon.

Yours sincerely,

James Swift

James Swift

enclosure

'Cold' Job Search Letter – To a Potential Employer (Teacher)

JANE SWIFT
18 Park Street, London X1 0BB
020 8123 4567   jane@address.co.uk

[Date]

Emily _____
Deputy Headteacher
ABC Primary School
Industry Square
London X2 2EF

Dear Ms _____,

> *'One hundred years from now, it will not matter what my bank account was,*
> *the sort of house I lived in, or the make of car I drove, but the world may be*
> *different because I was important in the life of a child.'* – anonymous.

If you are seeking a dedicated, resourceful teacher who not only has a background in teaching but an ability to truly inspire children, then we have an excellent reason to meet.

Often referred to as a *'kid magnet,'* I possess an extraordinary ability to relate to children and foster an environment of trust. This unique ability not only establishes a creative and stimulating classroom environment, but also encourages self-esteem and new heights of awareness among children of all ages.

Children are my passion. As a mother and a teacher, I have dedicated my life to being committed to the standards and practice, care and education of young people. For the past 10 years, I have worked extensively with my own children, through home schooling opportunities as well as with the LEA as a substitute teacher. In addition, I own and operate a company called Music Patch, which offers a distinctive programme designed to teach music to children in small focused groups. Here, I am instrumental in developing self-expression and creativity among children.

My long-term goal is to establish a theatre school to use my extensive theatre training, which I received at London University. Currently, I am enrolled on the MEd – Primary course at London University.

In today's society we face many challenges and cultural diversity. Families are often broken or dysfunctional, making it even more essential for our educational system to establish a positive effect in the lives of children. As an educator, committed to the mission that all children deserve an equal opportunity to excel, I offer you incredible value as a teacher, including knowledge, background and a remarkable drive to make a difference. My contribution to your school system would create a powerful impact on the lives of children. I look forward to meeting you to discuss your needs.

Yours sincerely,

Jane Swift

Jane Swift

'Cold' Job Search Letter – To a Potential Employer
(Electrical Engineering)

Jane Swift
18 Park Street, London X1 0BB
020 8123 4567   jane@anyaddress.co.uk

Phillip _____   [Date]
[Title]
ABC Ltd
Industry Square
London X2 2EF

Dear Mr _____,

My electrical engineering background, specifically my successes working on many defence, combat and Navy projects, is the chief asset I would bring to a position in your firm.

I understand that the primary function is to provide guidance for Navy TAURUS-I systems in electromagnetic environmental effects, shock and vibration, antenna blockage, and radar cross-section. I am thoroughly familiar with Navy acquisition programmes in general, and I have also dealt almost exclusively with Navy civilian and uniformed personnel throughout my career, so I am well-versed in Navy project specifications, requirements and protocol.

In my current position as Senior Systems Engineer for XYZ plc, a firm dealing primarily in Navy contracts, I supervise the software systems and testing associated with the FALCON Weapon System. And as the Chief Consulting Engineer with Consultant Associates, I deal with not only Navy security classification issues, but also those involving the Ministry of Defence.

Previously, as the manager of Development & Special Projects Test Engineering for DEF, I participated in the development of the Navy's AMBIT Test and Evaluation Master Plan for the AMBIT Acquisition Programme. While working with the AMBIT Combat System Integration and Test Team, we produced the first operating AMBIT class Combat System within extremely short time constraints, an accomplishment which led to the successful completion of the MOD milestone event.

My strengths are not only in development, but also in testing and analysis. Again, at DEF, when faced with the loss of data during an initial shock trial of the FALCON cruiser, I developed the following solution: we located video cameras at key equipment indicator panels and display consoles. The equipment recorded the data processes, which I then analysed and suggested corrective action. A similar video recording technique was used to solve a problem on the TAURUS-I antenna.

I believe my Navy and electrical engineering background is a quality match for the requirements stated for a position in your organization. Kindly review my CV, then please contact me at your earliest convenience to schedule a professional interview.

Yours sincerely,

Jane Swift

Jane Swift

'Cold' Job Search Letter – To a Potential Employer (Pharmaceutical Sales)

JAMES SWIFT
18 Park Street, London X1 0BB
020 8123 4567   james@anyaddress.co.uk

Emily _____   [Date]
[Title]
ABC Ltd
Industry Square
London X2 2EF

Dear Ms _____,

I currently hold a sales management position for a very successful retail company. My talents to achieve high sales volume, work cooperatively with diverse personalities, and focus on providing exceptional customer service have allowed me to excel in customer relations and succeed in sales and marketing.

I have always enjoyed a challenge and have made the decision to extend my experience to the pharmaceutical sales field. Pharmaceutical sales has been an interest of mine for some time and I am confident that my background and skills in customer service, human relations and product distribution would transfer well into pursuing this change. What I may lack in specific experience in your business, I more than make up for with my dedication, energy and determination.

I thoroughly understand the importance of developing customer relations, generating revenue from sales potential within a designated territory, and maintaining accurate customer information. I have the aptitude and willingness to learn the necessary technical medical materials to promote your products. I am fully capable of projecting a positive and professional image of an organization and its products, and I strongly believe I possess the necessary skills and qualifications your organization seeks to be successful in this field of work.

Your time in reviewing my confidential CV is greatly appreciated. I will follow up next week to answer any questions you may have regarding my qualifications. At that time, I would like to discuss the possibility of setting up a personal interview at a time to suit you. Please contact me if you would like to speak sooner.

Very truly yours,

James Swift

James Swift

enclosure

'Cold' Job Search Letter – To a Potential Employer (Recruiter)

James Swift
18 Park Street, London X1 0BB
020 8123 4567   james@anyaddress.co.uk

[Date]

Alice _____
[Title]
ABC Executive Search Consultants
Industry Square
London X2 2EF

Dear Ms _____,

Having spent several years as an executive recruiter, I realize the number of CVs you receive on a daily basis. However, I remember how valuable a few always turned out to be.

The purpose of this communication is to introduce myself and then to meet you with a view to joining your organization.

When asked which business situations have been the most challenging and rewarding, my answer is the time spent in the search profession.

My background, skills and talents are in all aspects of sales and sales management. My research indicates that your expertise is in this area.

I have enclosed a CV which will highlight and support my objectives. I would appreciate the opportunity to meet and exchange ideas. I will ring you over the next few days to make an appointment. If you prefer, you may reach me in the evening or leave a message on 020 8123 4567.

Thank you and I look forward to our meeting.

Sincerely,

James Swift

James Swift

enclosure

'Cold' Job Search Letter – To a Potential Employer (Project Management)

JAMES SWIFT
18 Park Street, London X1 0BB
020 8123 4567   james@anyaddress.co.uk

[Date]

Mr _____
ABC Ltd
Industry Square
London X2 2EF

Dear Mr _____,

Information technology expertise, combined with visionary leadership and the ability to motivate cross-functional teams and develop cost-effective solutions are key to creating long-term customer satisfaction and loyalty.

As a seasoned **Project Manager** experienced in providing strategic direction in the design and deployment of technology solutions, I have:

- Successfully managed customer accounts from defining project requirements through implementation.
- Engineered e-commerce business solutions for myriad organizations from start-up ventures to Blue Chip companies.
- Completed all of the coursework, including specialized electives, to obtain the Microsoft Certified Systems Engineer designation.
- Developed comprehensive RFIs and RFPs; selected the most qualified, cost-effective vendor; and directed cross-functional teams to ensure on-time, on-budget implementation.
- Efficiently prioritized projects, developed realistic timelines, and consistently met deadlines.
- Compiled and drove ratification of product requirements.
- Provided technical expertise to sales teams to assist them in closing the sale.

Could your company use a high achiever with a thirst for growth and new challenges? If so, I would like to discuss how my skills and experience could benefit your organization.

I look forward to speaking to you.

Sincerely,

James Swift

James Swift

enclosure

XYZ Newsletter

Whereas he worked as a Network Technician and Hardware Technician prior to his service as Deputy Director of IT for XYZ ... he **served with distinction** as IT director from 1997 to 2000; and ... **managed the correction** of the organization's complex year 2000 compliance-related issues **long before they became 'issues'** in 1996; and ... established long- and short-term **technological strategic 'vision'** and goals for the organization and conducted negotiations with outside vendors/contractors that **saved taxpayers hundreds of thousands** of pounds; and ... is **client-oriented** and **self-directed**, tireless and dedicated in the pursuit of a goal, has demonstrated the ability to **efficiently prioritize** projects and set schedules and deadlines, and can **assess potential problem areas and implement solutions** ...

Charley Henson

Drew Smith

'Cold' Job Search Letter – To a Potential Employer (Publishing)

JAMES SWIFT
18 Park Street ● London X1 0BB
020 8123 4567   james@anyaddress.co.uk

[Date]

Phillip _____
[Title]
ABC Ltd
Industry Square
London X2 2EF

Dear Mr _____,

In the interest of exploring opportunities in the publishing industry, I have enclosed my CV for your review.

Over the last two years, I have gained valuable knowledge and experience in many aspects of personnel assistance, office procedures and administrative operations. Recently I volunteered my time to edit a cookbook and have been responsible for editing the newsletter for my college. I consider myself a good writer and an avid reader and have always wanted to get into publishing. With my considerable energy, drive and ability to work long hours, I believe I could make a positive contribution to your organization, and I would appreciate the opportunity to discuss my qualifications with you.

Should any questions arise regarding the information on my CV, or if you need personal references, please do not hesitate to contact me at the address or telephone number shown above.

Thank you for your time and consideration. I look forward to meeting you.

Yours sincerely,

James Swift

James Swift

enclosure

'Cold' Job Search Letter – To a Potential Employer (General)

JANE SWIFT
18 Park Street, London X1 0BB
020 8123 4567   jane@anyaddress.co.uk

[Date]

Emily _____
[Title]
ABC Ltd
Industry Square
London X2 2EF

Dear Ms _____,

I am very interested in obtaining a position with your organization. Enclosed please find my CV for your review.

You will find most of the necessary background information contained in my CV. However, I would like to mention that I am available for immediate employment. I am also exploring the job market to obtain a position with a firm that will appreciate my skills and willingness to work eagerly with other people. I can definitely offer you longevity.

As my CV indicates, I am a Filipina and only arrived in the UK in 19— after my marriage to a UK citizen. I hope that this will explain my limited work record in this country. Also, English is the second language in the Philippines. It is spoken from childhood and is taught from grade one in school, so I am fluent in the language. Frankly, all I need to prove my abilities is an employer in need of an employee who is used to hard work and who has a strong work ethic.

I would like very much to arrange a personal interview where we can discuss my enthusiasm and qualifications for a position with your organization. I can be reached at the address and telephone number shown above.

Thank you for your time; I look forward to a favourable response.

Sincerely yours,

Jane Swift

Jane Swift

enclosure

'Cold' Job Search Letter – To a Potential Employer (International Sales)

JANE SWIFT
18 Park Street, London X1 0BB
020 8123 4567   jane@anyaddress.co.uk

[Date]

Phillip _____
[Title]
ABC Ltd
Industry Square
London X2 2EF

Dear Mr _____,

I received your name from Mr _____ last week. I spoke to him regarding career opportunities with _____ and he suggested contacting you. He assured me that he would pass my CV along to you; however, in the event that he did not, I am enclosing another.

As an avid cosmetics consumer, I understand and appreciate the high standards of quality that your firm honours. As you can see from my enclosed CV, I have had quite a lot of experience in the international arena. My past experience working overseas has brought me a greater understanding of international cultures and traditions, as well as a better understanding and appreciation of our own culture. These insights would certainly benefit a corporation with worldwide locations, such as your own. In addition, I have gained first-hand experience in the consumer marketplace through my various sales positions. I have noticed your recent expansion into the television media and am sure that an energetic individual would be an asset to ABC in this as well as other projects.

I would very much like to discuss career opportunities with ABC. I will be ringing you within the next few days to set up an interview. In the meantime, if you have any questions I may be reached at the number above. Thank you for your consideration.

Sincerely,

Jane Swift

Jane Swift

enclosure

Power Phrases

Consider using adaptations of these key phrases in your 'cold' letters to potential employers.

My twenty-two-year operations management career with a multi-billion-pound _____ company has been at increasing degrees of responsibility. While I have spent the last five years in top management, I am especially proud of my record – I started as a driver many years ago and, like cream, have risen to the top. I have consistently accomplished all goals assigned to me, particularly overall cost reductions, improved productivity, and customer service. Some of my achievements are: ...

Your recent acquisition of the _____ chain would indicate an intent to pursue Southeastern market opportunities more vigorously than you have in the past few years. I believe that my retail management background would complement your long-term strategy for _____ very effectively.

With the scarcity of qualified technical personnel that exists today, it is my thought that you would be interested in my qualifications as set forth in the attached CV.

In approximately three months, I am moving to _____ with my family, and am bringing with me fifteen solid years of banking experience – the last eight in branch operations management. I would like particularly to make use of this experience with your firm.

I have noticed that you conduct laser exposure testing at your facility. If there is a need for laser technicians in this enterprise, I would like to be considered for a position.

As you can see from my CV, I am a psychology graduate and was president of our debating society in my final year. I feel both would indicate a talent for sales. I did some selling in my summer job in 20 – (ABC Books), and found not only that I was successful, but that I thoroughly enjoyed it.

The position you described sounds challenging and interesting. After receiving your comments about the job requirements, I am convinced that I can make an immediate contribution towards the growth of _____ and would certainly hope that we may explore things further.

The opportunity to put to use my medical knowledge as well as my English degree would bring me great pleasure, and it would please me to know that I was bringing quality to your company.

I feel that the combination of _____'s educational environment and my desire to learn as much as possible about the data processing field could only bring about positive results.

If you think after talking to me and reading my CV that there might be an opportunity with your client company, I would be very interested. I have been put in many situations where I had to learn quickly, and have always enjoyed the challenge.

My accomplishments include: …

As my CV indicates, I have demonstrated commitment to clients and to my employer's goals. That track record is consistent in my career endeavours as well as in my life as a whole. I dedicate myself to whatever task is at hand, marshal my resources and stay with the project until it is completed – to my satisfaction. Since my goals and demands are even more stringent than my employers' expectations, I consistently exceed quotas and objectives.

You will notice one common thread throughout my career – I am an administrator and a problem solver.

Currently I am considering opportunities in the £40-£50K range.

My confidential CV is enclosed for your review and consideration.

My current salary requirement would be in the mid-to-high £30Ks, with specifics flexible, negotiable, and dependent upon such factors as benefit structure and advancement opportunity.

Having spent several years as a _____ , I realize the number of CVs you receive on a daily basis. However, I remember how valuable a few always turned out to be.

I would like the opportunity to discuss with you how we could mutually benefit one another. You may leave a message on my answering machine at my home and I will return the call. I look forward to hearing from you very soon.

I'm a clear communicator equally at ease with senior management, government officials and control agencies, vendors and contractors, and the construction/labour force. I'm a hard-driving manager who is project driven and is accustomed to inspiring the best job performance possible from associates and employees. I'm also creative enough to be in compliance with agency requirements without sacrificing profit or deadlines.

This job does seem to be the right challenge for me; I know that with my strong Java skills and manufacturing background experience I would be an asset to your company.

Hoping to meet you in person, I thank you for your time.

I will be ringing you on Friday, – August 20– to be sure you received my CV and to answer any questions you might have.

I have enclosed a CV that will highlight and support my objectives. I would appreciate the opportunity to meet and exchange ideas. I will ring you over the next few days to make an appointment. If you prefer, you may reach me in the evening or leave a message on 020 8123 4567.

'Cold' E-mail – To Employment Industry Professional (IT Professional)

Dear Mr _____,

Capitalizing on my success managing IT design and implementation projects for ABC Design in London, I am seeking a professional opportunity where my project management, customer relations and organizational skills could benefit your clients. With this goal in mind, I have attached for your consideration a CV outlining my qualifications.

Some of the experiences I would bring to a position with your firm include:

- Defining project parameters, including interviewing clients to assess goals and objectives, and developing specifications and project deliverables.
- Serving on leadership teams that have managed project budgets of up to £10 million to meet customer deadline requirements and budgetary constraints consistently.
- Coordinating activities of programmers, Web developers, software engineers, network engineers, graphic artists and customer representatives to meet project goals.
- Testing and validating applications during development stages and upon completion to ensure client objectives are met.

I am open to relocation anywhere in the United Kingdom and would eagerly accept either contract assignments or permanent employment. I believe that my capabilities would allow me to serve your needs and benefit your clients, and I would enjoy meeting you to discuss my qualifications in greater detail. Please contact me via phone or e-mail to arrange an initial interview.

Thank you for your time and consideration. I look forward to speaking to you soon.

Sincerely,

Jane Swift
020 8123 4567
jane@anyaddress.co.uk

'Cold' E-mail – To Employment Industry Professional (Technician)

Dear Ms _____,

My background inspecting power supplies for ABC and government contracts, along with my professional training in electronics engineering technologies, are among the chief assets I would bring to the position of Technician.

For eight years I was the Lead Product Assurance Inspector for XYZ, where I worked on several notable projects, including the Defence Meteorological Space Platform and the Mars Observer. My work involved not only component and complete assembly inspections, but also documentation, testing, and collaboration with ABC and government inspectors.

My CV shows that I have completed several ABC certifications, and I hold a degree in Electronics Engineering.

I am confident that my technical background equips me well for success in the technical position you have available. Kindly review my CV, then please contact me to arrange a professional interview.

Very truly yours,

James Swift
020 8123 4567
james@anyaddress.co.uk

'Cold' E-mail – To Employment Industry Professional (Computer Professional)

Dear Ms _____,

My broad background in all aspects of computers, from design and installation through to user training and maintenance, coupled with my business operations expertise, are the assets I would bring to a position with one of your clients.

Currently I hold a management level position with ABC, a firm that designs and builds flight simulators for UK and foreign governments. I provide the electronics expertise in completing approximately 12 major projects annually, which means I conceptualize the simulators' computerized mechanisms, direct the design and manufacturing processes, and then install and test the systems at clients' sites around the globe.

In addition to providing technical expertise, the other major aspect of my job involves aggressively targeting new business. At a point when ABC was facing an essentially saturated UK market, I designed and implemented an Internet Web site, and then had it translated into several languages to target international clientele. The site generated 80% of our new business within one year.

Other assets I would bring to this position include skill in relocating entire company computer systems from existing facilities to new or expanded sites, as well as experience servicing all major brands of PCs. I am extremely familiar with nearly every computer-associated component, program and operating system on today's market.

Thank you in advance for taking a few moments to review my CV. I am confident that the experience you'll find outlined therein will be valuable to your firm. Kindly contact me to arrange a professional interview.

Best regards,

James Swift
020 8123 4567
james@anyaddress.co.uk

'Cold' E-mail – To Employment Industry Professional (Programmer/Analyst)

Dear Ms _____,

My certification in computer programming, along with my professional background in electro-mechanical engineering, are among the primary assets I would bring to a programmer/analyst position with one of your clients.

As part of my training at Computer Institute in south London, I was required to design, write, code, edit and modify an e-commerce Web site. The project succeeded not only because of my skill in applying my technical knowledge, but also because of my strict attention to detail.

Currently I'm employed at ABC in London, executing experiments on electrical/mechanical equipment I was involved in manufacturing to ensure conformance to customers' specifications.

I am also committed to furthering my professional education, which is essential for success in this field. I plan to augment my knowledge by attending and completing relevant courses.

I am confident this background equips me well for success with one of your clients. Kindly review my CV, then please contact me to arrange an interview.

Very truly yours,

James Swift
020 8123 4567
james@anyaddress.co.uk

'Cold' E-mail – To Employment Industry Professional (Technology Project Manager)

Dear Mr _____,

As a highly proficient and experienced project manager with a passion for technology, I am routinely faced with challenges and the need to evaluate diversified programmes and their ability to meet operating requirements.

As you will note, my CV may not look like others you receive. My CV is beyond reciting job titles and duties – it reveals results. Having a complete picture of my expertise and experience is very important. For several years, I have spearheaded and developed various programmes to meet organizational needs.

I possess solid experience in systems integration, hardware and software analysis, and systems life cycle management. In addition to my managerial and technical experience, I will offer your company decisive leadership, dedication, and commitment to excellence.

The attached CV is submitted in confidence. I prefer that my present employer not be contacted until a position is officially offered. Your time and consideration are appreciated. I will contact your office next week to follow up and answer any questions you may have. Please feel free to contact me if you would like to speak sooner.

Sincerely,

James Swift
020 8123 4567
james@anyaddress.co.uk

'Cold' E-mail – To Employment Industry Professional (IT Management)

Dear Mr/Ms _____,

Leading information technology projects for high-growth companies is my area of expertise. Throughout my career I have been successful in identifying organizational needs and leading the development and implementation of industry-specific technologies to improve productivity, quality, operating performance and profitability.

In my current position at XYZ company, I have initiated and managed the technological advances, administrative infrastructures, training programmes and customization initiatives that have enabled the company to generate over £3 million in additional profits in the past year. The scope of my responsibilities has included the entire project management cycle, from initial needs assessment and technology evaluations through to vendor selection, internal systems development, beta testing, quality review, technical and user documentation, and full-scale, multi-site implementation.

My technological and management talents are complemented by my strong training, leadership and customer service skills. I am accustomed to providing ongoing support and relate well to employers at all levels of an organization, including senior executives. Most notable are my strengths in facilitating cooperation among cross-functional project teams to ensure that all projects are delivered on time, within budget, and to specification.

Originally hired for a one-year contract at XYZ, I have been offered a permanent position within the company. However, I am interested in greater challenges and would welcome the opportunity to meet you to determine the contributions I can make to your client. I will call you next week to set up an appointment.

Sincerely,

James Swift
020 8123 4567
james@anyaddress.co.uk

'Cold' E-mail – To Employment Industry Professional (Systems Integration)

Dear Company Representative,

My solid background in electrical engineering supported by extensive management and product development experience are key assets that I can contribute to your client's future success.

Throughout my career I have worked with cutting-edge technologies, including **embedded microprocessors**, **RF**, **telecommunications** and **wireless**, in the development and manufacture of products for varied industries. In all of my positions, integrating software, firmware and hardware to create unique applications has been a key strength. Some of these applications that proved quite marketable include development of custom instrumentation and a PC-based network for tracking vehicles in transit. In addition, I have also played an important role in both the sales and customer support process, helping ABC Ltd win its largest municipal contract with the City of London.

Currently, I am exploring opportunities in the telecommunications industry where I can contribute significant expertise in systems integration. I would welcome the opportunity to meet you to explore areas of mutual benefit. Attached is my CV for your review.

In order to present my credentials more fully, I will follow up with a call to you to answer any questions you may have. Thank you for your consideration.

Sincerely,

Jane Swift
020 8123 4567
jane@anyaddress.co.uk

'Cold' E-mail – To Employment Industry Professional (IT/IS Management)

Dear Mr _____,

In today's turbulent market, it can be difficult to find a highly skilled MIS professional with strong leadership, management and interpersonal skills. If you seek such a candidate who is ready for change, we have good reason to meet. Please find my CV attached for your review and consideration for an IT/IS management position.

I possess extensive experience in both management and Information Technology/ Information Systems. I also possess numerous certifications from both Novell and Microsoft and have become an expert in network design, installation and administration. I have been recognized and awarded for my technical abilities and top performance. In addition, my leadership skills stretch across management and team environments. For the past nine years I have successfully managed technical professionals, including training, leading, motivating and building high-performance teams. My management abilities have led to significant cost savings and new business for my employers. Also, I possess a BSc in Information Systems Management and am currently pursuing my Master's degree in MIS.

After meeting me, I think you'll agree I possess the necessary qualifications to lead an IS department into the future. I would appreciate the opportunity to discuss with you how I could make a quick and valuable contribution to your organization. I will ring you next week to set up a meeting. In the meantime, please don't hesitate to contact me for more information.

I look forward to meeting you in the near future. Thank you for your time and consideration.

Sincerely,

James Swift
020 8123 4567
james@anyaddress.co.uk

'Cold' E-mail – To Employment Industry Professional (Systems Administrator)

Dear Ms _____,

If you seek a new Systems Administrator who is not only technically oriented but also people oriented, then we have good reason to meet. As you'll find on my attached CV, I possess extensive technical skills and experience. What are more difficult to portray in a brief CV are my people skills.

Several colleagues, supervisors, subordinates and end-users have commended me for my interpersonal skills. I am dedicated to helping others with their technical issues and sharing my knowledge to help them complete their work more efficiently. My job is to serve as a support person, there to keep the system operating smoothly for end-users, as well as to provide them with training. I also understand that most technical projects are a team effort. Again, I have been recognized for my abilities as a team player as well as a team leader. I have a proven track record in taking projects and running with them, but the successes are a result of the combined efforts of the whole team. Whether it's a matter of motivating others, coordinating tasks, or just doing my part, I can do it.

My technical skills speak for themselves. My primary focus has been on Windows NT. In fact, I am currently pursuing my Microsoft Certified Systems Engineer qualification. My plans are to attain this at about the time I leave the Army. I will be able to bring this added expertise to an employer.

A meeting would be greatly appreciated. Please feel free to contact me to arrange a time or to gain further information on my background. I am sure you will agree that I am right for the job after reviewing my CV and meeting me in person.

Thank you for your time and prompt reply. I look forward to meeting you in the near future.

Best regards,

James Swift
020 8123 4567
james@anyaddress.co.uk

'Cold' Job Search Letter – To Employment Industry Professional (Project Management)

JANE SWIFT
18 Park Street, London X1 0BB
020 8123 4567   jane@anyaddress.co.uk

[Date]

Phillip _____
[Title]
ABC Ltd
Industry Square
London X2 2EF

Dear Mr _____,

ABC Ltd is well known to professionals throughout the region as the leading customer service recruitment company; it also maintains a strong reputation as a great employer. Your organization has created an environment in which people can excel, which is why I write to you today.

I present to you my skills, achievements, proven leadership and demonstrated ability to achieve quality and bottom-line results. I possess extensive experience in project management, system implementation, operations management and client relations. I have restructured and turned around a struggling department, achieved top levels of customer and employee satisfaction, and greatly improved the company edge in the market. This has been rewarded with promotions and a reputation for getting the job done. Briefly, some of my accomplishments include:

- As Global Customer Support manager of XYZ Solution Centre, I formed a global support office. I supported, staffed, directed, and streamlined the Solution Centre, resulting in an increase in customer satisfaction from 20% to 80%.
- As a Project Coordinator, I structured and established standard operating procedures for system implementation, turning a very dissatisfied customer into a customer who implemented the company Warehouse Management System in more than 15 sites.
- As a Project Implementation Manager for the 'Societe des Alcool de Quebec', I worked with a foreign government agency, communicating effectively in the customer's language and defusing many conflicts between all parties. I provided an exemplary Implementation Requirement Document, used by the company as a template in later projects.
- I designed, developed, tested, and implemented an Intelligent Computer Aided Instruction system using new learning concepts that was recognized by the LEA and helped the company in getting the funds needed.
- As operations manager at Utility Management, I automated and improved productivity levels to a record high through motivation and re-engineering of the entire operations.

I am confident that I can provide similar benefits to one of your clients as a member of your management team. I would appreciate the opportunity to meet you to determine how I can contribute to your company's future success.

Thank you for your consideration and reply. I look forward to meeting you and your team.

Sincerely,

Jane Swift

Jane Swift

enclosure

'Cold' Job Search Letter – To Employment Industry Professional (Internet Sales and Marketing)

Jane Swift
18 Park Street, London X1 0BB
020 8123 4567   jane@anyaddress.co.uk

[Date]

Phillip _____
[Title]
ABC Ltd
Industry Square
London X2 2EF

Dear Mr _____,

A start-up company is only as good as the people behind it, and when you're in the Internet arena you need people who are experienced and knowledgeable in this quickly growing and ever-changing medium. I believe one of your searches is over if you seek an entrepreneurial-minded Sales & Marketing professional with expertise in formulating, managing and marketing new Internet services.

As my enclosed CV briefly summarizes, I possess hands-on experience in starting an Internet-based venture. This background encompasses all aspects of starting a business – market research, business plan development, investor financing, marketing and sales, and more. I also have an excellent track record in sales, including lead generation, cold calling, presentation delivery and closing. Additional strengths include:

- **Communication skills** – As a financial consultant, I marketed to top-level executives and business owners with net worths in the millions. This required the ability to communicate on their level and explain complex terms in their language. Also, seven years of teaching has honed my communication as well as leadership skills. In addition to my Physics degree, I hold a Post Graduate Certificate of Education.
- **Analytical skills** – Earning a Bachelor's degree in Physics required numerous courses that were intense in analysing subject material and drawing educated conclusions. Progressing my way through the ranks in the financial industry also involved strong analytical ability, as I had to evaluate several investment vehicles to ensure I offered the most appropriate ones to my clients. Finally, during the start-up of my company, I performed extensive market and competitor analysis, along with financial analysis.
- **Perseverance** – There are many areas in my background that give evidence of my perseverance. Graduating with a Physics degree from a well-known university is one. Becoming one of the top financial consultants on my special team with XYZ is another: I started at the bottom and worked my way up, learning as I went along. When I wasn't reaching my goals, I dedicated myself to learning new skills and honing existing ones in order to achieve success. Also, being an entrepreneur requires commitment and perseverance to succeed.

I think you'll agree after reading the enclosed CV and meeting me in person that I have the qualifications you seek for your Sales & Marketing Manager position. I would appreciate the opportunity to meet you to discuss how I might benefit one of your clients. I will call you next week to arrange a time. In the meantime, please feel free to contact me for further information.

I look forward to meeting you in the near future. Thank you for your time and consideration.

Yours sincerely,

Jane Swift

Jane Swift

enclosure

'Cold' Job Search Letter – To Employment Industry Professional (Executive Computer Specialist)

James Swift
18 Park Street, London X1 0BB
020 8123 4567   james@anyaddress.co.uk

[Date]

Emily _____
[Title]
ABC Ltd
Industry Square
London X2 2EF

Dear Ms _____,

My experience installing and maintaining computer networks, hardware and software, along with my skills in training users and developing cost-saving applications, are the assets I would bring to the position of Executive Computer Specialist.

I am a Certified Novell Administrator. My technical skills include expertise in Novell Netware, MS DOS and Windows, as well as experience with hardware including Cabletron, and software including the Microsoft Office Suite.

My computer expertise has saved my employers production time and costs. As a Senior Computer Specialist, I installed a Personal Computer LAN using the Novell Netware Networking System. I saved £20,000 and used the savings to upgrade the equipment installation. Also in that position I designed and implemented a system to cut printing costs. The system is projected to save the government £2.5 million over four years.

I have also developed software packages, including 'point of sale' software and mortgage software, which was for commercial sale.

I believe my skills and experience would make me succeed in the position of Executive Computer Specialist. Kindly review my CV, then contact me to arrange a professional interview.

Yours sincerely

James Swift

James Swift

enclosure

'Cold' Job Search Letter – To Employment Industry Professional (Director)

Jane Swift
18 Park Street, London X1 0BB
020 8123 4567   jane@anyaddress.co.uk

[Date]

Mr _____
[Title]
ABC Ltd
Industry Square
London X2 2EF

Dear Mr _____,

In the course of your search assignments, you may have a requirement for an organized and goal-oriented Director. My present position provides me with the qualifications and experience necessary to successfully fulfil a Director's position. Key strengths which I possess for the success of an administrative position include:

- Direct line operations responsibility improving gross margin to 8.0%.
- Planning and developing over £10 million in new construction projects.
- Reduction of departmental operating expenses to 1.1% below budget.
- Negotiating and developing contractual arrangements with vendors.

I have the ability to define problems, assess both large-scale and smaller implications of a project, and implement solutions.

The enclosed CV briefly outlines my administrative and business background. My geographic preferences are the South and Southeast regions of the country. Relocating to a client's location does not present a problem. Also, I possess an MBA degree from _____ University, and a BSc in Business Administration from _____University. Depending upon location and other factors, my salary requirements would be between £80,000 and £100,000.

If it appears that my qualifications meet the needs of one of your clients, I would be happy to discuss my background further in a meeting with you or in an interview with the client. I will be contacting your office in the near future to determine the status of my application.

Yours sincerely,

Jane Swift

Jane Swift

enclosure

'Cold' Job Search Letter – To Employment Industry Professional (Senior Manager)

James Swift
18 Park Street, London X1 0BB
020 8123 4567   james@anyaddress.co.uk

[Date]

Mr _____
ABC Ltd
Industry Square
London X2 2EF

Dear Mr _____,

Mentored by Bob _____, founder of _____, I successfully progressed within his privately held organization for twelve years, serving on the **Board of Directors of 13 separate companies** and holding positions including **Treasurer**, **Director of Finance** and ultimately **CEO**. During my tenure the company grew from 7 employees to more than 1,000 while **revenues increased from £2 million to £65 million**. My enclosed CV gives further details.

My reason for contacting you is simple. I am interested in exploring any senior management opportunities that may be available through your organization and would also be interested in interim or consulting roles. Geographically speaking, I have no limitations and am available for relocation throughout the UK and abroad. Due to the level and quality of my performance I feel it pertinent to state that I am only willing to consider positions consistent with my current income level. I have the experience, the talent and the energy to turn around, create or grow a dynamic organization.

I have built my career on my commitment and ability to create open lines of communication between the Board of Directors and senior management to **protect the investments of my organization** and to **assure the attainment of the target return**.

I look forward to hearing from you in the near future to discuss any mutually beneficial opportunities. If you do not at present have a need for a professional with my experience but know of someone who may, please be so kind as to pass on my letter and CV to that individual, or simply ring me.

Yours sincerely,

James Swift

James Swift

enclosure

'Cold' Job Search Letter – To Employment Industry Professional (International Operations)

James Swift
18 Park Street, London X1 0BB
020 8123 4567   james@anyaddress.co.uk

[Date]

Ms _____
[Title]
ABC Ltd
Industry Square
London X2 2EF

Dear Ms _____,

Over the years, I have built a successful career in **international operations and project management** on my ability to assess situations accurately and quickly, identify problems and focus on strategies that obtain results. I am currently seeking a challenging opportunity with an internationally focused, growth-oriented organization. I am willing to explore interim assignments and consulting projects as well as senior management opportunities. My enclosed CV details some of my accomplishments and credentials.

I have extensive experience in **diplomacy and international public affairs** dealing with foreign government officials, Heads of State and Ambassadors as well as senior executives. Building effective teams and inspiring others to peak performance are among my strengths. I am particularly adept at living and working effectively in foreign countries and with individuals of various cultural backgrounds. As such I am interested in opportunities both in the UK and abroad.

Feasibility studies, **crisis resolution** and **international risk assessment** are areas where I excel. Unit construction and operations, mining/drilling and industrial equipment procurement, sales and distribution are areas where I may be of particular assistance, but my skills are transferable to virtually any industry.

I look forward to hearing from you to discuss any mutually beneficial opportunities that you may be aware of. Please feel free to send my CV to others who may have a need for a professional of my calibre.

Yours sincerely,

James Swift

James Swift

enclosure

Power Phrases

Consider using adaptations of these key phrases in your 'cold' letters to employment industry professionals.

I am an optimist, thrive on challenges, lead by example and readily adapt to situations. If your client – international or domestic – would benefit from these kinds of qualities, we should get to meet each other. If you would ring or write at a time convenient to you, I look forward to telling you more about my background.

As a dedicated listener, I am usually designated for client/customer relations and produce notable results in client/customer retention – even under the least favourable conditions.

An industry association referred to _____ as an active and selective executive search firm, and mentioned your name because of your work in logistics. I liked that referral and think our meeting would be mutually beneficial.

I would like to talk to you personally to further discuss our meeting. I suggest next week, the week beginning – October, when you have a free minute. I have asked my staff to forward your message immediately in case I am unavailable when you call. I look forward to hearing from you.

Please include my name in your job search database.

Including a mortgage loan benefit, I am currently earning £3,000 per month plus a car allowance. This should provide you with an indication of my present job level. Your suggestions or comments would be appreciated.

For 25 years, my family operated one of the most prestigious landmark inn/restaurants in Dorset. From the age of 6, I was a part of the family workforce – I couldn't wait to 'help.' That attitude pervades my work ethic and I'm grateful for the training that helped me to develop an attitude of service, teamwork and pride in performance and product.

One of your clients is looking for me, if not today then sometime in the near future. I know good people are hard to find because I've had to find them myself.

I have the depth of experience it takes to make a positive contribution.

Income is in the mid-five figures, but the right opportunity is the motivating factor. References and CV are available. With my well-rounded professional background I look forward to a new and interesting career opportunity through your firm.

I'm a natural 'enroller' because my enthusiasm is contagious and I personally project credibility – people are inclined to (1) cooperate and participate wholeheartedly on projects with which I'm involved, (2) favourably consider products I recommend, and (3) be open to my efforts on their behalf when they experience problems or dissatisfaction.

The following are some highlights of my track record for your consideration: ...

I understand your clients frequently ask you to locate senior operating executives with much higher than average ability to accomplish difficult jobs quickly and profitably.

It is my goal to play an integral part in the development, operation and success of a small to mid-sized company where the diversity of my experience and the level of my commitment can be used to their fullest advantage and I can have the satisfaction of seeing the results of my efforts ... a real impact on profitability!

Please call at a time convenient to you this week so we can explore potential opportunities more fully. Use the home number, please; our company's uncertain financial status is stirring up the office rumour mill. Thank you for your time and attention.

I am a motivated and dedicated leader. Many of my staff have worked for me for 10 to 30 years. My enthusiasm for meeting goals and accomplishing _objectives has been contagious, and I know how to reward outstanding performance without disturbing a profit and loss balance. My employees and I thrive on a 'family' environment with no loss of respect or production._

As a former business owner, I am well aware of the needs, concerns and challenges facing management. By the same token, I am accustomed to operating with the best interests of the total business in mind – and at heart, as well. I operate expeditiously, constantly seeking the best use of time, effort, resources and money … for my staff and myself.

My experience as an entrepreneur as well as an employee of a powerful, demanding employer gives me the unique ability to empathize with the needs of management as well as the assertiveness necessary to represent management effectively.

I'm seeking an opportunity to join an employer who can benefit from my expertise and experience while offering me the opportunity for challenge and continued professional growth, as well as commensurate compensation.

I'm a dedicated listener and an accomplished problem solver, always seeking to assist clients in achieving their mission. My clients experience and express a sense of trust and confidence in me and my recommendations because my sincerity and my efforts invested on their behalf are evident and consistent. They never have a doubt that I really care and will operate in their best interests.

Broadcast E-mail (Senior Buyer/Purchasing Agent/Purchasing Manager)

Mr / Ms _____:

SENIOR BUYER * PURCHASING AGENT * PURCHASING MANAGER

Do you cringe at the high costs your company incurs for goods and services?

Do you need someone who will maximize vendor resources, working hard to secure lower-cost, longer-term contracts?

Do you need someone on board who will immediately slash supply costs and streamline purchasing operations?

  With more than 20 years in purchasing, retail sales management, store expansions, and new product research and market launch, I believe I may offer just what you're missing.
  In my esteemed career with ABC, a premier auto parts and accessories distributor, I have:

- Directed procurement of over £100M of goods and services, accounting for 60% of ABC's total purchasing budget.
- Launched 3 private label programmes, garnering £500k in additional profits during the first year of distribution.
- Recouped £300k in stolen merchandise and prosecuted the employees responsible.
- Generated £3M in savings by cultivating partnerships and negotiating long-term contracts with key suppliers.

  With the right opportunity, I'd be perfectly willing to relocate. With regard to salary, I understand that flexibility is essential and would consider a compensation package appropriate for a person with my outstanding qualifications and dynamic track record of accomplishments.
  If you're tired of seeing your company's profits slip through your fingers, ring me today to arrange a business meeting. I can't wait to discuss how I could benefit your purchasing operation right away. I can be reached at the number below to arrange our interview.

Yours faithfully,

James Swift
020 8123 4567
james@anyaddress.co.uk

Broadcast E-mail (Operations)

Dear Human Resources Administrator:

Perhaps your organization is seeking a take-charge individual to manage multifaceted clothing production and distribution operations with direct responsibility for overseeing all aspects of yarn purchasing, delivery schedules, staff management and vendor relations, along with many other areas too extensive to mention on one page. If this is the case, then you will want to consider me as a viable candidate.

I bring with me fourteen years of solid experience, a Bachelor's degree, and a lot of common sense that goes a long way in this industry. Currently in my eighth year of dedication with ABC Ltd in the capacity of Yarn Manager, I continue to prove myself as a professional highly capable of wearing many hats in a fast-paced manufacturing environment.

In addition to my ability to manage a broad scope of daily operations, I have played an instrumental role in the development and implementation of a multimillion pound computerized system that has greatly improved productivity levels, reduced unnecessary spending, and improved overall communication in the workplace. Combined with my ability to lead, motivate and train direct reports, multilingual communication skills that include fluency in Spanish and German, and a talent for making sure the job gets done right, I am confident that I would be an asset to your management team.

Although the accompanying CV illustrates my background well, I feel that a personal interview would better demonstrate my knowledge and abilities. Therefore, I would appreciate the opportunity of an interview with you at a convenient time. Thank you for your review and consideration. I look forward to hearing from you soon.

Yours sincerely,

Jane Swift
020 8123 4567
jane@anyaddress.co.uk

Broadcast E-mail (New Product Marketing)

Dear Mr _____,

If you are looking for a successful executive to take charge of new product marketing, you will be interested in talking to me.

Ten years of experience in every aspect of marketing and sales in different industries give me the confidence to be open to opportunities in almost any field. My search is focused on companies that innovate, because I am particularly effective at new product marketing. I have successfully managed new product-marketing research, launch planning, advertising, product training and sales support, as well as direct sales. In my current position with XYZ Company, I created several products and marketing approaches on which other operating divisions in the company based their programmes.

My business education includes a Marketing MBA from _____ University's School of Management, and provides me with a variety of useful analytical tools in managing problems and maximizing opportunities. My superior sales track record guarantees that I bring the reality of the marketplace to each business situation; I know what sells and why.

Currently, my total compensation package is in the low fortiess; I am looking for a company that rewards performance consistently.

Since I am currently weighing several interesting opportunities, please contact me immediately if you are conducting any searches that might be a good fit. Relocation is no problem.

Thank you in advance for your consideration.

Yours sincerely,

James Swift
020 8123 4567
james@anyaddress.co.uk

Broadcast E-mail (Senior Marketing Executive)

Dear Mr _____ ,

I recently learned of your firm's excellent record of matching senior marketing executives with top organizations. I have also learned that you have an officer-level marketing assignment in process now – I am a serious candidate for your client's vacancy. Please consider some successes:

- After joining _____ as Marketing Director, I revitalized a declining processed-meat product category in less than a year, introducing better-tasting formulas and actually reducing product costs by over £100,000. Dramatic new packaging enhanced customer appeal, and fresh promotion strategies doubled previous sales records.
- I have carefully crafted and fine-tuned many new product introductions and line extensions, such as _____ turkey, _____ processed meats, and _____'s deodorant maxi-pads.
- My sales/marketing experience dates from 1990, when I formed a direct sales company to pay for my _____ MBA (now the top-rated programme in the UK, I'm proud to say). Much of my subsequent success springs from strong working relationships with sales management and joint sales calls with field reps and marketing brokers. I have designed events like the _____ programme, and _____'s sponsorship of the City football team.
- I have a strong personal and professional interest in consumer electronics. I consult professionally and have successfully adapted marketing techniques for home and commercial satellite systems, 'high-tech' audio/video, and radio communications equipment.

Please inform your client I am fluent in French and I quickly absorb other languages. If your client challenges executives with the greatest of responsibilities and rewards them for remarkable performance, please contact me as soon as possible. I'll quickly repeat my past successes.

Sincerely,

Jane Swift
020 8123 4567
jane@anyaddress.co.uk

Broadcast E-mail (Director, Asset Liquidation)

Dear Mr _____,

In recent years, as the Director of Lease Asset Liquidation with XYZ UK, I successfully engineered the recovery of £23 million in assets, almost three times the original buyout offer of £8 million. Throughout my career I have been instrumental in developing and implementing workout and liquidation strategies and as such I have earned a strong reputation as a professional who gets the job done.

My reason for contacting you is simple. I am interested in project opportunities that will serve both to challenge and to make use of my abilities in asset liquidation management. My current project will be completed within the next four to six weeks. I am currently considering offers and intend to make a decision by 1st February.

The attached summary details some of my accomplishments. I look forward to hearing from you to discuss any mutually beneficial opportunities. Please feel free to pass along my CV to others who may have a need for my professional assistance.

Sincerely,

James Swift
020 8123 4567
james@anyaddress.co.uk

Broadcast E-mail (Healthcare Manager)

Dear Ms _____,

Recently I was hand-picked to prospect new business in an expansion territory. By creating a new 'communication loop' I was able to stimulate product awareness. This resulted in a 500% increase in business participation and generated more than £2.4 million in annual revenues. As a result of my performance I have received four promotions in just 36 months. My attached CV itemizes my credentials.

As you are probably aware, however, XYZ Healthcare is soon to merge with Anycorp; and although I know I will have a solid place with the company subsequent to the merger, I feel the time has come for me to look at other opportunities. Due to the level and quality of my performance (I more than doubled my income last year and will do the same this year) I feel it pertinent to state that I am only willing to consider positions that will allow me to be compensated appropriately.

I trust that you will treat this correspondence, as well as my CV, with utmost confidentiality. I look forward to hearing from you in the near future to discuss any mutually beneficial opportunities – which need not necessarily be in the healthcare area.

Sincerely,

James Swift
020 8123 4567
james@anyaddress.co.uk

Broadcast Letter (Database Engineer)

Jane Swift
18 Park Street, London X1 0BB
020 8123 4567 jane@anyaddress.co.uk

[Date]
Phillip _____
[Title]
ABC Ltd
Industry Square
London X2 2EF

Dear Mr _____,

   Empowering your employees with the information and tools necessary to make better strategic business decisions is very likely to improve your company's competitive advantage and profitability. I can do this through insightful strategic planning and the delivery of superior data warehouse and decision support systems.

   My extensive career experience in data warehousing, database administration and business systems development, coupled with my commitment to exceed customer expectations and my focus on achieving sustainable strategic competitive advantage, are the primary assets I would bring to your Director of Database Engineering position. I have successfully delivered numerous data warehouse projects that were effectively aligned with company strategic objectives. I am also highly skilled at directing teams on complex initiatives and improving processes, communication, teamwork and quality.

   As a senior-level employee of XYZ Information Technology Ltd, I have established an excellent track record for successfully managing large complex projects. Notably, I managed a £10 million development project for Business One, building and implementing their first enterprise data warehouse and certain downstream divisional data marts. So successful was this project that within three months after implementation it established itself as the recognized supreme source of accurate company data for all of Business One's North European business units. Additionally, it met tight service level commitments over 97% of the time and experienced no downtime due to programming error.

   As a Project Leader/Manager for DEF Business Systems Ltd, I also managed the development of a large data warehouse. I led the design and development efforts for this data warehouse of sales information for their Speciality Products division. This was the first data warehouse developed at DEF that successfully met user expectations.

   An additional asset I would bring to your organization is competency in correlating data warehousing functions with overall company goals. I am skilled in providing advice to senior managers and executives and adept at monitoring data warehouse systems to continually ensure their value and usefulness to an organization as a whole.

   I am confident that this experience equips me well for success as your Director of Database Engineering. Kindly review my CV, then please contact me to arrange a professional interview.

Yours sincerely,

Jane Swift

Jane Swift

Broadcast Letter (Senior Technical Sales)

JAMES SWIFT
18 Park Street, London X1 0BB
020 8123 4567   james@anyaddress.co.uk

Emily _____   [Date]
[Title]
ABC Ltd
Industry Square
London X2 2EF

Dear Ms _____,

As a seasoned Technical Sales and Marketing Consultant, I've generated considerable new business for my previous employers, and now I'd like to do the same for you. For the past 15 years I have pursued an increasingly successful career in telecommunications sales and marketing. Among my accomplishments are:

SALES
Qualified to spearhead the entire sales cycle management process, from initial client consultation and needs assessment through to product demonstration, price and service negotiations, and final sales closings.

MARKETING
Success in orchestrating all aspects of developing a gainful marketing strategy, from competitive market intelligence and trend analysis, product development, launch and positioning, to distribution management and customer care.

TELECOMMUNICATIONS & NETWORK SOLUTIONS
Recognized for pioneering technology solutions that meet the needs of complex customer service, logistics and distribution operations. Able to test operations to ensure optimum systems functionality and availability, guide systems implementation across multiple platforms, and deliver user training and support programmes that outpace the competition.

I hope you will contact me in the very near future. You'll find my address and telephone number above. I would welcome the opportunity to contribute my skills to the success of your marketing team and look forward to learning about any available opportunities in your company.

Yours sincerely,

James Swift

James Swift

enclosure

Broadcast Letter (Senior R&D Engineer)

JAMES SWIFT
18 Park Street, London X1 0BB
020 8123 4567   james@anyaddress.co.uk

SENIOR R&D ENGINEER ... patent holder ... launched x number of new products ... recognized worldwide ... created win-win alliances ... cornered global markets ...

[Date]

Phillip _____
[Title]
ABC Ltd
Industry Square
London X2 2EF

Dear Mr _____,
If your R&D-to-market time needs a sense of urgency, creativity and a seasoned coordinator of people and priorities, I am one individual you need to discuss the ABD POSITION with. Here's why:

- STRATEGIC PLANNING: Etched long- and short-term technological plans that kept a £2B manufacturer ahead of its competition since 1999
- COORDINATED RESOURCES: 20+ years in planning, reviewing, and benchmarking technical performance, meeting budgetary goals and coordinating interlaboratory and interdepartmental efforts
- IGNITED STAFFS' CREATIVITY: Led efforts and piqued an in-house multidisciplinary R&D staff's synergy; got x number of new products to market
- ENRICHED KNOWLEDGE: Trained sales, marketing and technical staffs since 1995; well-known for abilities to communicate new ideas, selected for numerous assignments in product training worldwide
- MOVED THE MARKET TO OUR PRODUCT: Recognized expert – created the need for leading-edge technology in the cutting tool market by featuring results in technical articles for major publications
- INTEGRATED OPERATIONS: 1 of 2 individuals to integrate a newly acquired company's R&D with parent company's
- IGNORED STIGMAS: First person to involve marketing with R&D – created pathway between R&D and marketing, bringing projects to market in record time; landed £6 million+ in new accounts – only non-salesperson to get a one-of-a-kind annual sales award
- IMPECCABLE RECORD: Achieved 70 to 80 per cent first-time success rate in field testing for all products developed; hold x number of UK patents; consulted worldwide by engineers and scientists; published; presenter at technical conferences since post-doctoral fellowship

Reviewing my credentials and past results, you will note they occurred in the XYZ field. However, I am confident the core *technical, interpersonal and organizational expertise I would bring to your staff and customers would easily retrofit at* ABC LTD.

– MORE –

James Swift
2 of 2

If you need *a driven problem solver who can get your people moving to the work*, I am readily available to discuss how I can channel my more than two decades of success as your ABD POSITION at ABC LTD. I will be in the area next month, and would prefer to meet you then.

I am in a position to move to the North West area, and *am ready to demonstrate how I could reignite your R&D efforts and create a flurry of opportunity.* Should you need added information, please do not hesitate to contact me on 020 8123 4567 or james@anyaddress.co.uk.

Sincerely,

James Swift

James Swift

enclosure

Broadcast Letter (Management)

Jane Swift
18 Park Street, London X1 0BB
020 8123 4567   jane@anyaddress.co.uk

[Date]

Phillip _____
[Title]
ABC Ltd
Industry Square
London X2 2EF

Dear Mr _____,

> **People will only give you what you're willing to accept. That's why my staff employed 'The Golden Rule' every day, treating customers the way they themselves would like to be treated.**

If you need someone with a technical background who has hired and kept top talent challenged and on their toes to deliver exemplary service, then consider that in 20+ years:

— I translated my knowledge of physics and business into profits and operational success – for my staff, my employer and myself.
— I took on the lead engineering position in my second year with an industry giant, skipping over the traditional 12-year career path – I simply outworked everyone and never said I couldn't do something or get it done on time or within budget.
— I earned full latitude in decision making after proving my team's understanding of a new target market's needs – I introduced more products than my predecessors, improved processes, and cut manufacturing and warranty costs by roughly £1M the first year.
— Operations I had an impact on experienced extremely low employee turnover – and employees met or exceeded customer expectations 100 per cent of the time.

I've made sure my staff are so service-oriented that the customer doesn't have to ask for warranty repairs or 'the next step' – they have the answers or already have performed the warranty work.

And when my name is on a project, it is always on schedule within budget – and is a winner:

— When a relationship with a speciality manufacturer ended, I spearheaded development of an intake manifold line, analysed and negotiated manufacturing costs, and selected vendors – and launched an 18-unit product line in 18 months that led the industry.
— The first race manifold we developed took the first 5 finishes in the 1985 motorsport race without prior testing by participating teams.

If you seek someone with the work ethic of a business partner, then I am your top choice for the _____ opportunity with ABC Ltd. I fully understand the nuts-and-bolts of customer service, and certainly can combine my financial know-how with proven success in the field at ABC.

Jane Swift
Page 2 of 2

Right now I'm ready to step down from entrepreneurial management, simplify my role, and do 'one or three things' well for an organization that values integrity, hard work and creativity.

If I sound like the person you need at ABC , then contact me right away to discuss the _____ opportunity. I can be reached on 020 8123 4567 after 6 pm. Monday to Friday, or at my place of business on 020 8345 6789 during business hours. I will take the liberty of contacting you on Monday at 10 am to see when we can arrange an interview.

Yours truly,

Jane Swift

Jane Swift

enclosure

Broadcast Letter (HR Generalist)

Jane Swift
18 Park Street, London X1 0BB
020 8123 4567   jane@anyaddress.co.uk

HR GENERALIST
9 years advising senior decision-makers on employee matters...
5 years in benefits administration for £1B company and 5 affiliates...
15 years delivering HR presentations...
Open enrolment/benefits processing for professional employees...
13 years grievance/disciplinary meeting involvement...
10+ years training/development, entry through professional levels...
Worked through mergers and reorganizations...
Created award-winning concept for enrolment booklet...
Earned highest ratings throughout career...

[Date]

Phillip _____
[Title]
ABC Ltd
Industry Square
London X2 2EF

Dear Mr _____,

If your organization seeks someone to advance your human resources programmes, consider my proven track record. I am ready for a challenge with ABC Ltd, as your recent growth needs someone used to working with new subsidiaries and maintaining the bottom line. I am absolutely ready to step in as your Human Resources Director at ABC, as my commitment extends to all areas you seek to address.

I bring you and your employees objectivity, knowledge of policy/procedure implementation and interpretation, and hands-on work in an ever-changing climate. Here are some highlighted abilities that could be put to work immediately at ABC Ltd:

— MET THE CHALLENGE: With little notification, stepped in and was an asset in an HR Directorship capacity; administered £12M in health and pension benefits; initiated multi-tier healthcare plan to better suit regional product needs

— BENEFITS: 5 years working with open enrolment for all levels of employees – restructured benefits during 3 internal reorganizations

— REMAINED FLEXIBLE: Adapted to the needs of entrepreneurial organizations while continuing a career with conservative major utility company

— LEADERSHIP: Entrusted to step in for superiors due to track record in HR; number 1 person consulted by senior managers of a £1B parent company and its 5 affiliates regarding HR or benefits; met with bargaining unit leadership, discussed and resolved grievances and complaints

Jane Swift
2 of 2

— COMMUNITY INVOLVEMENT: Accepted leadership role in major charity organization, keynote speaker for regional fund-raising appearances

— TRAINING / DEVELOPMENT: Delivered HR and benefits presentations since 1995, safety training, 2 years

— OVER/ABOVE: Travelled over 3-year period to help a newly formed company whose explosive growth took them to 2,000 employees in 3 years (coordinated staffing and benefit enrolment while maintaining existing workload); singled out for HR support for special finance division structure, took on policy making/interpretation and HR

If you need someone seasoned in policy making who can interface with decision-makers and keep you 100 per cent compliant with regulations, I am awaiting your call for an interview.

I prefer to take the lead in contacting you, so I will call on Monday at 10 am to brief you on how my background could be an immediate asset and arrange our meeting. I can forward a CV for your review immediately. Should you need to reach me earlier, I am on 020 8123 4567.

Sincerely,

Jane Swift

Jane Swift

~ Benefits Enrolment ~ Multi-Tier Coverage ~ Labour Relations ~ Grievances ~ Arbitration ~
Job Bidding ~CPP, CRS, PDS ~ Redundancy Compensation ~
Sexual Harassment ~ Safety Training ~ Background Investigations ~

Broadcast Letter (Operations Manager)

JAMES SWIFT
18 Park Street ● London X1 0BB
020 8123 4567 james@anyaddress.co.uk

[Date]

ABC Ltd
Industry Square
London
Attention Ms Emily_____

Dear Ms _____,

Do you need an experienced, versatile individual who can improve bottom-line profits? I can offer innovative ideas to the position of Operations Manager – ideas that can benefit a service-driven, quality-oriented company like yours. No one has money to burn in a tough economy, which is why adding an already-skilled manager to your staff can reduce time and money.

The match between your needs and my talents is ideal. Why? Because my strengths lie in understanding the labour and manufacturing operations that design, build, install and manage equipment for environmental and production improvements. I am a leader both by example and through effective management of individuals and teams. In short, I have the drive and vision to make a positive difference in any organization.

Dozens of proposed projects have been successfully implemented due to my established reputation for the quality of work completed. The work performed under my direction has come in at, or below, budget and we meet project deadlines.

The enclosed CV summarizes my qualifications and achievements. I would be glad to discuss any of this information with you as an opportunity of employment. Because 'proven skills' are best explained in person, I look forward to our conversation and will ring early next week to arrange our meeting. Thank you for taking the time to review my CV and for your consideration.

Sincerely,

James Swift

James Swift

enclosure

Broadcast Letter (Information Technology Programme Manager)

James Swift
18 Park Street, London X1 0BB
020 8123 4567   james@anyaddress.co.uk

[Date]

Mr Philip____
CIO
ABC Ltd
Industry Square
London X2 2EF

Dear Mr _____,

May I ask your advice and assistance?

As a result of XYZ's merger with DEF, I am confidentially exploring my opportunities. Although I am confident that I will be offered a role in the new organization, I am currently assessing where I can make the optimal contribution.

I am an Information Technology Programme Manager. In this role, I have led the development of key financial systems and strategic business plans, co-managed the seamless migration of two divisions to another site, and founded the City People Networking Group – delivering noteworthy cost savings and productivity gains. For the past 11 years, I've had dream jobs with leading firms like GHI and JKL. I have been entrusted with the direction of large-scale, global projects. Many times, I learned 'on my feet' – to implement new systems, design testing methods, manage resources, repair damaged vendor relations for mutual gain and to meet a wide array of challenges. My career has accelerated based on the results, as you'll note from the accomplishments in my enclosed CV.

I'm considering transferring my skills and experience to an organization where I can continue to be a team player and visionary leader for state-of-the-art technology programmes, and where I'll also continue to learn new functional and technical areas. My expertise and interests are in the financial service industry.

I would greatly appreciate a few minutes of your time to discuss my options and glean any suggestions you can offer. I'll phone you in a few days to see if we can arrange a brief meeting.

Thanks very much.

Yours sincerely,

James Swift

James Swift

enclosure

Broadcast Letter (Director of Operations)

James Swift
18 Park Street   ●   London X1 0BB
020 8123 4567   james@anyaddress.co.uk

[Date]

Philip_____, [Title]
ABC Ltd
Industry Square
London X2 2EF

Dear Mr _____,

Problem – Action – Results. It is a simple formula, and one that I have implemented successfully throughout my long career in manufacturing. A former business associate passed your name on to me after commenting that my business philosophy and style reminded him of a CEO he had heard speak at a conference in Manchester. That CEO was you.

It has been several years since I took my first job as a machinist back in Norwich, but I have never lost my enthusiasm for finding faster and better ways to accomplish goals while cutting costs. I have worked my way up through the ranks from Foreman, to Plant Supervisor, to Manufacturing Engineer, to Assistant Director of Operations, and finally Director of Operations. Taking a swing at every new idea that came my way, I may have missed a few, but overall my batting average has been good:

- led a £200M manufacturing firm to earning ISO 9002 certification on first attempt;
- revitalized operations at a plant site in Scotland by implementing a comprehensive employee training programme;
- increased profits by 200% by identifying and rectifying problems with production and delivery at a Sheffield manufacturing facility;
- spearheaded technological advances at an Oxfordshire plant which was converting from manual to CAD/CAM capabilities.

I believe strongly in teams and am comfortable working with R&D, engineering and marketing professionals. My colleagues have expressed appreciation for my direct and honest approach to people and problems.

Between jobs now, I am available on 20th March and would like to get together with you to explore potential opportunities with ABC. It would be great to meet over lunch. I will give you a ring on the morning of the 18th to see if that can be arranged.

I'm sending along my CV to lay a foundation for our discussion. I look forward to meeting you and exchanging ideas.

Sincerely,

James Swift

James Swift

enclosure

Broadcast Letter (Consultant)

JAMES SWIFT
18 Park Street, London X1 0BB
020 8123 4567   james@anyaddress.co.uk

[Date]
Philip _____, [Title]
ABC Ltd
Industry Square
London X2 2EF

Dear Mr _____,

- **Is your organization fully prepared to safeguard its technology services, information and facilities in the event of a disaster?**

- **Are you taking full advantage of high-value and cost-effective vendor agreements?**

- **Do you benefit from high team performance and low turnover?**

If you have answered 'No' to any of the above questions, then allow me to introduce myself and the expertise I can offer your organization. With a proven and award-winning track record of achievement, I offer a unique combination of expertise in disaster recovery/business continuity planning, vendor management/negotiations, and team leadership. I am currently offering my services to organizations within the London area, and would like to draw your attention to the value I offer.

Put simply, my expertise is delivering results. In previous positions, I have designed, implemented and optimized comprehensive world-class disaster recovery and information security procedures, saved millions in vendor negotiations and third-party service agreements, and led a variety of cross-functional teams to consistently achieve and exceed organizational mandates.

If the following interests you, I invite you to review the attached CV which further illustrates my experience, achievements and expertise:

- **Expert in Disaster Recovery, Information Security and Business Continuity** – expertise includes planning, protection and offsite recovery of technology services, databases and facilities

- **Superior contract procurement, negotiation and vendor management capabilities** – proven record for negotiating agreements that improve service quality and save millions in vendor costs

- **Strong, decisive and motivating leader** – reputation for building and leading high-performance teams to breakthrough achievement

- Available for **full-time, part-time, contract and consulting opportunities**

If you believe that you could benefit from a highly motivated and talented professional with a reputation for generating results, then I would welcome the opportunity to meet and discuss the specific value I can offer your organization.

I thank you for your consideration and I look forward to speaking to you soon.

Sincerely,

James Swift

James Swift

enclosure: CV

Broadcast Letter (Project Manager)

JANE SWIFT
MBA, PMP
18 Park Street, Lonon X1 0BB
020 8123 4567   jane@anyaddress.co.uk
– WILLING TO RELOCATE –

[Date]

Dear Employer:

Because of current market conditions and high unemployment, I am sure you have many candidates and few **Project or Training Manager** positions to fill. With this letter and CV, please allow me to add to your group; but, may I also give a few reasons why you might want to call me ahead of other qualified candidates should an appropriate position become available?

You will note that my educational and professional **background is broad** and includes experience in post-secondary organizations, community colleges, business and the armed forces. Because of this range of experience, I am able to bring **insight and the ability to relate well to individuals at all levels and from diverse backgrounds.**

Working within for-profit organizations has enabled me to develop an **eye for the bottom line**. Whether it be budgetary or profit-enhancing, I am continually evaluating systems and methods to make them more efficient and productive.

Incredible as it may sound, I appreciate and welcome change. I am **known for my abilities as a change agent**. However, while I may embrace change – technological or otherwise – I recognize that many do not. Therefore, from a management standpoint, I look for ways to make transitions more tolerable for the people in my charge.

While my CV is comprehensive, it does not fully demonstrate the manner in which I have achieved success. My character, personality and the ability to effectively lead a project or team could be best seen in a personal meeting. Therefore, I would welcome an interview to further discuss your needs and my qualifications. Thank you for your time and consideration.

Yours faithfully,

Jane Swift

Jane Swift

enclosure

Power Phrases

Consider using adaptations of these key phrases in your broadcast letters.

I hope this summary describes my experience and provides you with a better understanding of my capabilities. Thank you for your help.

If you feel that any of the strengths outlined in my CV could make a valuable contribution to your organization, please contact me to let me know of your interest.

Recently I read about the expansion of your company in the _____. As the _____ industry is of great interest to me, I was excited to learn of the new developments within ABC Ltd.

I feel confident that a short conversation about my experience and your growth plans would be mutually beneficial. I will be ringing you early next week to follow up this letter.

Currently, my total compensation package is in the low £40s; and I am looking for a company that rewards performance consistently.

I'm a responsive and responsible listener, maintaining a gracious and empathetic attitude, creatively troubleshooting, thoroughly researching options and making well-thought-out recommendations designed to establish and enhance customer/client relationships.

I am available for relocation and travel and am looking for compensation in the £30K range.

I fervently request more than your cursory consideration; I request your time to verify my claims. YOUR TIME WILL NOT BE WASTED.

Superior recommendations from industry leaders as well as verifiable salary history are available.

I hope you will not think me presumptuous in writing directly to you; however, in view of your position, I believe that you are more aware of your organization's telecommunications personnel requirements than anyone else.

I am confident that with my experience I can make a significant contribution to your organization.

Throughout my career, I've been fortunate to represent quality merchandise and services and have learned just how to present them in their most favourable light. I know how to evaluate competition, to assess consumer/market needs, exploit a market niche, maximize profit margins, and create and maintain a reputation for dependability and excellent service.

I am a self-starter looking to join a reputable firm, one that could benefit from an individual who is ready to give 110 per cent. With over three years of sales experience, I have developed excellent interpersonal, organizational and communication skills. I am a hard-working individual who is motivated by the knowledge that my earnings are directly related to the time, energy and effort that I commit to my position.

I am personable, present a highly professional image, and deal effectively with both peers and clientele. I am confident you will agree that I should be representing your firm and not your competition. My salary requirements are negotiable. I will ring you this week to set up a mutually convenient time for an interview.

Since beginning with ABC Company, my average commission has progressed from £250 to £400 a week. My current salary or commission requirement would range upward of the mid-£20ks, with specifics flexible and negotiable.

I look forward to hearing from you in the near future to arrange an interview with you, during which I hope to learn more about the position, your company's plans and goals, and how I can contribute to the success of your team.

I am grateful for that environment and the faith that was demonstrated in my capabilities. I automatically moved into the role of Executive Assistant, constantly seeking ways to limit expenses, cut costs and generate additional profit for the company. I was exceptionally successful in that endeavor – while managing 5 operations, 3 warehouses, 6 Warehouse Managers and a staff of 60.

I appreciate the time you've spent reviewing this letter (and the accompanying material). I hope to hear from you in the very near future to arrange to meet in person and discuss just how my qualifications may be of value to your organization.

Networking E-mail (HR Administration)

Dear _____,

It was a pleasure to speak to you on the telephone recently and, even more so, to be remembered after all these years.

As mentioned during our conversation, I have just recently re-entered the job market and have ten years of experience with a 3,000-employee retail organization in the area of human resources administration. My experience includes recruitment and selection, human resources planning and employee relations. I have been responsible for all facets of management of the company personnel, including development and training, and liaison with both staff and training providers.

My goal is to become an HR Manager in a larger organization with the possibility of advancement in the Human Resources area. My preference is to remain in the South East.

For your information, my CV is attached. If any situations come to mind where you think my skills and background would fit or if you have any suggestions as to others to whom it might be beneficial for me to speak, I would appreciate hearing from you. I can be reached on the telephone number shown below.

Again, I very much enjoyed our conversation.

Yours truly,

James Swift
020 8123 4567
james@anyaddress.co.uk

Networking E-mail (Publishing)

Dear _____,

It was a pleasure to meet you for lunch today. I am grateful for the time you took out of your busy schedule to assist me in my job search.

It was fascinating to learn about the new technology which is beginning to play a major role in the publishing field. I have already been to the book shop to purchase the book by _____ which you highly recommended. I look forward to reading about his 'space age' ideas.

I will be contacting _____ within the next few days to set up an appointment. I will let you know how things are progressing once I have met her.

Thanks again for your help. You will be hearing from me soon.

Yours sincerely,

James Swift
020 8123 4567
james@anyaddress.co.uk

Networking E-mail (Administrative Assistant)

Dear _____,

_____ suggested that I contact you regarding employment opportunities.

After many years in the legal community, I have decided that a career change is due in order to use my interpersonal skills to their fullest. As you may know, a secretary/paralegal position offers little advancement unless you become a lawyer or move into the administrative areas. It is with this growth potential in mind that I desire to work with upper-level management in a corporate environment as an administrative assistant or executive secretary.

I am sending as attachments for your review a copy of my CV and letters of recommendation. I look forward to the opportunity of meeting you soon. I have recently resigned from _____ and may be contacted on my home phone number, below. Thank you.

Very truly yours,

Jane Swift
020 8123 4567
jane@anyaddress.co.uk

Networking Letter (Management)

JANE SWIFT
18 Park Street, London X1 0BB
020 8123 4567   jane@anyaddress.co.uk

[Date]

Philip_____, [Title]
ABC Ltd
Industry Square
London X2 2EF

Dear Mr Harmond,

It has been said, *'in today's world there are two kinds of companies – the quick and the dead'.* I propose the same is true of managers. I am a dynamic management professional with extraordinary team-building and interpersonal skills, and thrive in a fast-paced environment that is constantly moving and producing solid bottom-line results. I relish a challenge and will never run from a difficult situation. In fact, if you want a successful completion, you can count on it, accurately, timely and right the first time.

In addition to solid people skills, I posses an extensive management background in International Affairs. While living in the Germany for five years, I had the opportunity to study the language and culture. Bilingual with excellent comprehension of both German and English, my translation skills are strong in both languages. I also have conversational knowledge of French. Having held direct responsibility for commercial dealings with the UK, Ireland, and Germany, my knack for capturing key client relations with diverse cultures and people is intense. I would like to bring my business savvy and management/marketing skills to your firm.

My experience spans industries such as Property Development, International Affairs and Procurement; however, I am an ideal candidate for a company that values a well-rounded person who can step in wherever needed and isn't afraid to learn. Dedicated to doing whatever it takes to achieve outstanding results, I would lead your team to meet tight deadlines. In short, I would not let you down.

My CV is enclosed for your consideration. I look forward to meeting you to discuss your needs and the immediate impact I would make on your organization.

Yours sincerely,

Jane Swift

Enclosure

Networking Letter (Sales/Marketing)

James Swift
18 Park Street, London X1 0BB
020 8123 4567   james@anyaddress.co.uk

[Date]

Philip_____, [Title]
ABC Ltd
Industry Square
London X2 2EF

Dear Mr _____,

A good friend of mine, Allen Austin, suggested that I contact you to introduce myself for potential employment. I have excellent credentials, but more than that, I love golf!

As you will see from the attached CV, my dynamic professional experience is extensive not only in sales, but also in customer service. I can be counted on to provide expertise in market identification and penetration, key account management, and superb customer relationship management. Above all, you can be assured of one thing – my extraordinary powers of persuasion will expand your revenues and increase your bottom line!

Hard work and determination have always paid off for me. Last year I was awarded **_Salesperson of the Year with over 47% increase in my territory_** encompassing most of the South of England. Even more exciting is the fact that this achievement came during a unique challenge and perhaps throughout one of the toughest years the industry has seen, as fuel prices skyrocketed and haulage companies were determined to keep expenses low. As the year reaches mid-point, I am averaging about a 32% increase and, once again, lead the sales team!

I am an excellent candidate for a sales position with ABC. Not only do I possess outstanding sales ability, tools and techniques, but, I have an intense determination to succeed despite the odds, much like a professional golfer. Above all, I have a compelling passion for the game of golf and would use this enthusiasm in the industry, making me relentless in obtaining market share as well as establishing and maintaining strong client relations for your company.

Since that first golf club cradled in my hand at the age of 11, golf has been a huge part of my life. Looking back and remembering how excited I would be to find 'extra' golf balls hidden behind the bushes and trees, NO surprise surpassed encountering an ABC ball. ABC has set the standard for quality for as long as I can remember. I have watched over the years as ABC has been at the pinnacle of innovation and new products. I offer my incredible passion and enthusiasm to you and am confident that our partnership would be one of long-term mutual benefit.

If you give me this chance, you will be guaranteed several things. That I will excel for you as I have for all the companies I have worked for, which are leaders in their industry; I will commit to aggressive hard work and a superior work ethic that will make you proud; and I will share my unique talent to build and keep relationships strong, which is truly my greatest asset. I will EARN the right to be in your circle, but more than that, I will NEVER let you down.

James Swift
Page 2 of 2

I look forward to meeting you and discussing further the immediate contribution and high impact I would make on your team.

Yours sincerely,

James Swift

Enclosure

Networking Letter (Chief Financial Officer)

JAMES SWIFT
18 Park Street ● London X1 0BB
020 8123 4567 james@anyaddress.co.uk

Dear _____,

Perhaps your company could benefit from a strong chief financial officer with a record of major contributions to business and profit growth.

The scope of my expertise is extensive and includes the full complement of corporate finance, accounting, budgeting, banking, tax, treasury, internal controls and reporting functions. Equally important are my qualifications in business planning, operations, MIS technology, administration and general management.

A business partner to management, I have been effective in working with all departments, linking finance with operations to improve productivity, efficiency and bottom-line results. Recruited at The XYZ Company to provide finance and systems technology expertise, I created a solid infrastructure to support corporate growth as the company made the transition from a wholesale-retail distributor to a retail operator. Recent accomplishments include:

- **Significant contributor to the increase in operating profits from under £400k to more than £4M.**
- **Key member of due diligence team in the acquisition of 25 operating units that increased market penetration 27% and gross sales 32%.**
- **Spearheaded leading-edge MIS design and implementation, streamlining systems and procedures that dramatically enhanced productivity while cutting costs.**

A 'hands-on' manager effective in building team work and cultivating strong internal/external relationships, I am flexible and responsive to the quickly changing demands of the business, industry and marketplace. If you are seeking a talented and proactive finance executive to complement your management team, I would welcome a personal interview. Thank you for your consideration.

Yours sincerely,

James Swift

Enclosure

Networking Letter (General)

JAMES SWIFT
18 Park Street, London X1 0BB
020 8123 4567   james@anyaddress.co.uk

[date]

Mr Philip_____
ABC Ltd
Industry Square
London X2 2EF

Dear Philip,

Congratulations on your re-election. I hope this letter finds you and your family well and that you have an enjoyable Christmas.

I am writing to update you on my job search. You may recall from our last discussion that I am now focusing on obtaining a position that will sustain me until such time as I am ready for retirement (in three to five years).

As you recommended, I have applications on file with ABC for various hourly-paid positions and have corresponded with various department heads, in each case indicating my flexibility and strong interest in making a meaningful contribution to smooth operations within one of their departments.

I genuinely appreciate the advice and assistance you have offered to date. Once again, I am requesting that if you are aware of any other avenues I should be pursuing, please let me know. I believe I have skills and experience to offer and can be an asset to someone in just about any position requiring maturity, reliability and dedication.

Thank you, again, for all you help, and 'Merry Christmas.'

Sincerely,

James Swift

Power Phrases

Consider using adaptations of these key phrases in your networking letters.

It was good talking to you again. As promised, I am enclosing a copy of my CV for your information. If any appropriate opportunities come to your attention, I would appreciate it if you would keep me in mind.

After you have had a chance to look over the CV, please give me a ring.

I am beginning to put some 'feelers' out in advance of the completion of my degree in December.

I do not intend to target any specific type of job. I am open to almost anything that my qualifications will fit. My only criteria are the following:...

I would appreciate any advice and/or referrals you might be able to give me.

I am looking for a position in management and would appreciate any assistance you could provide.

As always, it was good to talk to you. Your positive outlook is catching. I've been called the eternal optimist, but I always feel more upbeat after a conversation with you.

Many thanks for the words of encouragement and taking the time from your busy schedule to help me. It is truly appreciated. I have never faced an unemployment situation like this before.

It was a pleasure to speak to you on the telephone recently and, even more so, to be remembered after all these years.

For your information, enclosed is my CV. If any situations come to mind where you think my skills and background would fit, or if you have any suggestions as to others to whom it might be beneficial for me to speak, I would appreciate hearing from you. I can be reached on the telephone numbers listed above.

He assured me that he would pass my CV along to you; however, in the event that it has not reached you yet, I am enclosing another.

Perhaps you know of a company that could use this scope of experience. In this regard, I enclose a copy of my CV outlining a few of my more significant accomplishments.

My objective is to find a _____ level position at a marketing-driven company where my skills can contribute to the firm's growth and profitability.

I am not limited by location and would consider the opportunity wherever it presented itself.

First of all, let me thank you sincerely for taking the time and trouble to return my call last Monday. I found our conversation informative, entertaining and (alas) a little scary. Needless to say, I genuinely appreciate your prompt response and generous, helpful advice.

Again, a thousand thanks for your time and consideration.
If I might ask you one last favour, could you please give me your opinion of the revision? A copy is enclosed.

I am writing to you in response to our recent conversation over the telephone. I thank you for your time and your advice. It was most generous of you and sincerely appreciated. Please accept my apologies for invading your privacy. I anticipated an address for written correspondence from an answering service.

I look forward to hearing from you on your next visit to _____.

I hope you'll keep me in mind if you hear of anything that's up my street!

_I recently learned that your firm is well-connected with manufacturers in the _____ area and does quality work. We should talk soon, since it's very likely we can help each other. I'll be in the office all next week and look forward to hearing from you. I have alerted my secretary; she'll put your call right through._

_____ suggested that I contact you regarding employment opportunities._

_After many years in the _____ community, I have decided that a career change is due in order to use my interpersonal skills to their fullest._

Follow-up E-mail (after telephone contact) (General)

Dear Ms _____,

I appreciate the time you took yesterday to discuss the position at _____. I recognize that timing and awareness of interest are very important in searches of this type. Your comment regarding an attempt to contact me earlier this summer is a case in point.

Attached, as you requested, you will find an outline CV. I also believe that my experiences as a director of physical plant services are readily transferable to a new environment. I believe that I can contribute a great deal to the satisfaction of your client's needs.

Realizing that letters and CV are not an entirely satisfactory means of judging a person's ability or personality, I suggest a personal interview to discuss further your client's needs and my qualifications. I can be reached directly or via message on 020 8123 4567, so that we may arrange a mutually convenient time to meet. I look forward to hearing from you. Thank you for your time and consideration.

Sincerely,

Jane Swift
020 8123 4567
jane@anyaddress.co.uk

Follow-up E-mail (after telephone contact)
(Arts Management)

Dear Ms _____,

As per yesterday's conversation, I am forwarding a copy of my CV and am looking forward to our meeting in the very near future.

As we discussed, the positions which interest me are as follows:

Event/Arts Management
Promotions/Advertising/Public Relations
Corporate Training

I am a fanatic about image, excellence and attention to quality and detail. As my academic and career background reveal, I have the tenacity of a terrier when it comes to task accomplishment.

I have never held a '9 to 5' job and would most likely be bored to death if I had one. Therefore, I am looking for something fast-paced and challenging to my grey matter that will allow growth and advancement and an opportunity to learn. I am in my element when I am in a position to organize … the more details the better!

I'll give you a call on Tuesday, — th March to try to arrange an appointment for further discussion.

Sincerely,

Jane Swift
020 8123 4567
jane@anyaddress.co.uk

Follow-up E-mail (after telephone contact)
(Telemarketing)

Dear Ms _____,

This letter is in response to our phone conversation this afternoon and your online job posting on CareerCity.com regarding the _____ position available.

My background includes experience (sales and technical) with a wide range of computer systems, as well as with industrial distributed process-control systems and measurement instrumentation. Considering the complexity of the equipment I've worked on and sold, most of the products being marketed by your organization will present no difficulty to me. The customer base would take a little time, but this would be nothing excessive.

I am a bright, articulate and well-groomed professional with excellent telemarketing skills, sales instincts and closing abilities. I would like to meet you to discuss how I could contribute to the effectiveness and profitability of your operations.

Sincerely,

James Swift
020 8123 4567
james@anyaddress.co.uk

Follow-up E-mail (after telephone contact) (General)

Ms _____ ,

As per my telephone conversation with Stephanie in your office today, this letter will confirm our meeting on Friday 9 June, 20— at 2.00 pm.

Again, thank you for your flexibility and for working out this meeting at a time convenient to me.

I look forward to continuing the discussion we had over the telephone in greater detail.

Very sincerely yours,

Jane Swift
020 8123 4567
jane@anyaddress.co.uk

Follow-up Letter (after telephone contact)
(Legal Assistant)

JANE SWIFT
18 Park Street, London X1 0BB
020 8123 4567   jane@anyaddress.co.uk

[Date]

Phillip _____
[Title]
ABC Ltd
Industry Square
London X2 2EF

Dear Mr _____,

Thank you for returning my telephone call yesterday. It was a pleasure speaking to you and, as promised, a copy of my CV is enclosed. As I mentioned, I have been working in law firms since the end of February, as well as working on weekends and in the evenings for over one year. At present, I am looking for a second or third shift to continue developing my word-processing and legal skills.

Although the majority of my positions have been more managerial and less secretarial, I have developed strong office skills over the years. While I was attending both undergraduate and graduate courses, I worked as an Administrative Assistant to Faculty and Department Heads, in addition to working in other professional capacities.

_____ speaks very highly of me, and if you need to confirm a reference with him, please feel free to contact him at _____. In addition, I would be happy to supply you with names of people I have worked for within law firms over the past year.

Within the next day, I will be contacting you to arrange a convenient meeting time to discuss the position you now have available. However, if you would like to speak to me, feel free to contact me on 020 8123 4567.

Thank you again for calling yesterday. I look forward to speaking to you on the telephone, and meeting you in person.

Sincerely,

Jane Swift

Jane Swift

enclosure

Follow-up Letter (after telephone contact)
(Advertising Sales)

Jane Swift
18 Park Street ● London X1 0BB
020 8123 4567   jane@anyaddress.co.uk

[Date]

Phillip _____
[Title]
ABC Ltd
Industry Square
London X2 EF

Dear Mr _____,

Thank you for taking the time recently to respond to my questions concerning a _____ position with _____, as advertised in _____ (— October, 20—). As you suggested, I have enclosed my CV for your review and consideration.

As you will find detailed on my CV, I offer nearly two years of sales experience, with over one year of successful advertising sales for a £l million regional business publication.

Within one year, I have developed a formerly neglected territory from approximately £50,000 to its current £180,000 in annual sales.

I have an excellent track record in customer retention, account penetration, low receivables and consistent goal achievement. I have had experience working with client advertising agencies and directly with smaller clients. I am confident that I can make similar contributions to your sales efforts, and would consider an interview with _____ to be a tremendous career opportunity.

As I have mentioned, I am relocating to your area in January and I would welcome the opportunity to discuss my background and accomplishments with you in further detail. I will be in your area on Friday, —th December, and will ring you early next week to see if we might arrange a meeting at that time.

Best regards,

Jane Swift

Jane Swift

enclosure

Follow-up Letter (after telephone contact)
(Purchasing)

James Swift
18 Park Street, London X1 0BB
020 8123 4567   james@anyaddress.co.uk

[Date]

Bob _____
[Title]
ABC Ltd
Industry Square
London X2 2EF

Dear Mr _____,

In reference to our telephone conversation, enclosed is my _____ CV. I believe the one you have is written with a purchasing position in mind.

Since we last spoke I have been working as a business consultant for the _____ group of companies on projects in a number of different areas outlined below.

- Spearheaded and supervised upgrading of the _____ companies' communications systems, including printing and copy machines, telecommunications systems, computer hardware and software systems, computer scanning system, computer filing system, and fax and modem transmission systems.
- Set up and implemented an auto and entry floor mat marketing programme for _____ including pricing and product displays for retail sales outlets.
- Researched, purchased and installed a bar code labelling programme for the companies' products, including label set-up and printing systems to allow them to sell their products to _____.
- Participated in the design and layout of a new logo for _____ division including specifications for all letterheads, forms and printed communications materials.
- Provided major input for a factory-paid _____ point-of-sale system to display custom automotive floor mats.

Most of my projects should be wrapped up by the end of November, and so I will be looking for another company that could make use of my broad range of experience. Please let me know if you think you might have something for me.

Sincerely,

James Swift

James Swift

enclosure

Follow-up Letter (after telephone contact)
(Merchandising)

JAMES SWIFT
18 Park Street, London X1 0BB
020 8123 4567 james@anyaddress.co.uk

[Date]

Bob _____
[Title]
ABC ltd
Industry Square
London X2 2EF

Dear Mr _____,

As you will recall, we spoke about my qualifications for the opportunity with your York client (account No. 5188), and you mentioned that you would be forwarding my CV for consideration.

I wanted you to have my updated CV, and I am enclosing several copies. I hope you'll send one to your client and keep another for your own files. I'm aware that you have many business leads and that my qualifications might pertain to other opportunities; please remember me if something arises that would tie in with my background.

My experience in grocery and merchandising areas is considerable, and I have an extensive network of business contacts in the North West. My many long-term professional relationships would benefit any employer in this area.

I'd like to meet you to tell you more about my background and to show you some of the training and marketing materials I've developed. This would give you a better picture of my capabilities.

I'll be in touch with you in the near future to find out when we might get together. Thank you again for your consideration.

Sincerely yours,

James Swift

James Swift

enclosures

Follow-up Letter (after telephone contact) (Manager)

James Swift
18 Park Street, London X1 0BB
020 8123 4567   james@anyaddress.co.uk

[Date]

Bob _____
[Title]
ABC Ltd
Industry Square
London X2 2EF

Dear Mr _____,

THANK YOU for allowing me to tell you a little about myself. I have just completed my MBA (December, 20 —) and would appreciate the opportunity to talk to your client companies who are in need of an experienced and seasoned manager. Whether the need is for general (operational) management, products, marketing or sales, my substantial background in management, marketing and technical products should be very valuable to your clients.

I have enclosed two CVs (marketing-oriented and operational-oriented) with some other information which you may find useful. With eyes firmly welded to the bottom line, I offer: the ABILITY to manage, build and quickly understand the business; EXPERIENCE in domestic and international corporate cultures; INTELLIGENCE and the capacity to grasp essential elements; and the WILLINGNESS to work hard, travel and relocate.

Realizing that most of your clients aren't looking for Directors, I'm not necessarily looking for fancy titles (but I am promotable). What I am looking for is that special position which will offer not only a challenge but a career opportunity with long-range potential. I know my successes will bring them (and me) rewards.

CVs and letters are brief by their very nature and cannot tell the whole story. I would be happy to discuss with your client and you how my commitment to them will help solve their needs or problems and will definitely make good things happen! After all, isn't that the bottom line?

May we work together?

Yours sincerely,

James Swift

James Swift

enclosures

Power Phrases

Consider using adaptations of these key phrases in your follow-up letters after phone calls.

As you requested in our telephone conversation this morning, I am enclosing a copy of my CV for your review.

As you can see from my CV, I have some excellent secretarial experience.

I'll give you a ring on Tuesday, —th March to arrange an appointment for further discussion.

In reference to our telephone conversation, enclosed is my sales and marketing CV; I believe the one you have is written with a purchasing position in mind.

I am a bright, articulate and well-groomed professional with excellent telemarketing skills, sales instincts and closing abilities. I am seeking a dynamic position with a reputable firm. I would like to meet you in person to discuss how I could contribute to the effectiveness of your clients' operations.

Again, thank you for your flexibility and for arranging this at a time convenient to me.

Please remember me if something arises that would tie in with my background.

My many long-term professional relationships would benefit any employer in this area.

I'd like to meet you to tell you more about my background and to show you some of the training and marketing materials I've developed. This would give you a better picture of my capabilities.

As you suggested when we spoke last week, I have enclosed my CV for your review and consideration. I contacted you on the recommendation of _____ of _____, who thought that you might have an interest in my qualifications for a position in the near future.

I have long admired _____ for its innovations in the industry, and I would consider it a tremendous career opportunity to be associated with your organization.

Follow-up E-mail (after face-to-face meeting) (General)

Dear Mr _____,

I appreciate the time you took today interviewing me for the position. I hope our two-hour meeting did not throw off the rest of the day's schedule. I trust you will agree that it was time well spent, as I sensed we connected on every major point discussed.

Your insight on e-commerce was intriguing. My history in hi-tech, manufacturing and biomedical industries and background in technology solutions seems to be a good match with the opportunities available in your company. As I mentioned, at XYZ Biomedical I initiated the marketing stratagems that opened our markets to the USA. What I failed to mention is that I also have contacts with some e-commerce investors developing online portals targeted to Americans.

I am very interested in the position and would like to contact you on Tuesday to see where we stand.

Sincerely,

James Swift
020 8123 4567
james@anyaddress.co.uk

Follow-up E-mail (after face-to-face meeting) (Sales Manager)

[date]

Mr. Philip_____
[title]
ABC Ltd
Industry Square
London X2 2EF

Dear Mr _____,

I thoroughly enjoyed our meeting on Wednesday. After learning more about ABC and its goals, the prospect of joining the organization as the Western Region Sales Manager is even more exciting.

One of the most important things I have learned in my 20+ years in sales is to listen to what the customer needs. I have always taken pride in designing customized solutions that not only meet the clients' objectives, but also are competitive in price. This philosophy has enabled me to exceed corporate expectations for 17 consecutive years. In addition, I have managed to convert about 65% of my clients to 'repeat order' accounts, an objective you indicated was a high priority for your sales team in ensuring the company's continued growth.

ABC's Western Region Sales Manager position is an important cornerstone in the company's overall growth plans for the new fiscal year. The company is poised to make significant strides to gain ground on the competition and the West of England territory will be instrumental in making the corporate goals a reality. I am excited about contributing my expertise, meeting ABC's customers, and building long-term client relationships.

Thanks again for your time. I am certain that I can be a valuable asset to your sales team, and I look forward to having the opportunity to contribute to ABC's growth.

Sincerely,

James Swift
020 8123 4567
james@anyaddress.co.uk

Follow-up E-mail (after face-to-face meeting) (Management)

Dear Mr _____,

The position we discussed on Friday is a tremendously challenging one. After reviewing your comments about the job requirements, I am convinced that I can make an immediate contribution towards the growth and profitability of ABC Ltd.

Since you are going to reach a decision quickly, I would like to mention the following points, which I feel qualify me for the job we discussed:

1. Proven ability to generate fresh ideas and creative solutions to difficult problems

2. Experience in the area of programme planning and development

3. Ability to successfully manage many projects at the same time

4. A facility for working effectively with people at all levels of management

5. Experience in administration, general management and presentations

6. An intense desire to do an outstanding job in anything which I undertake

Thank you for the time and courtesy extended to me. I will look forward to hearing from you.

Sincerely,

James Swift
020 8123 4567
james@anyaddress.co.uk

Follow-up E-mail (after face-to-face meeting) (Graphic Design)

Dear Mr _____,

It was a pleasure speaking to you regarding my search for a position in ABC Graphic Design. Thank you for your initial interest.

The position I am looking for is usually found in a corporate marketing or public relations department. The titles vary: Graphic Design Manager, Advertising Manager and Publications Director are a few. In almost every case the job description includes management and coordination of the company's printed marketing materials, whether they are produced by in-house designers or by an outside advertising agency or design firm.

I would like to stay in the _____ area; at least, I would like to search this area first. My salary requirement is £_____ a year.

My professional experience, education, activities and skills uniquely qualify me for a position in ABC Graphic Design. My portfolio documents over eight years of experience in the business, and includes design, project consultation and supervision of quality printed material for a wide range of clients.

I hope you will keep me on your files for future reference. I will telephone your office next week to discuss my situation further.

Sincerely,

James Swift
020 8123 4567
james@anyaddress.co.uk

Follow-up E-mail (after face-to-face meeting) (General)

Dear Ms _____,

It was a pleasure meeting you last week in your office. I appreciate the time you spent with me, as well as the valuable information you offered. As we discussed, I have adjusted my CV in regard to my position with _____. I have attached the new CV with this e-mail so that your files can be updated.

_____, please allow me to thank you again for the compliment on my ability to handle an interview well. Please keep this in mind when considering me for placement with one of your clients.

Sincerely,

Jane Swift
020 8123 4567
jane@anyaddress.co.uk

Follow-up E-mail (after face-to-face meeting) (Auditing)

Mr _____,

Thank you for allowing me the opportunity to meet you to discuss the EDP Audit position currently available at ABC. The position sounds very challenging and rewarding, with ample room for growth. I feel my background and qualifications prepare me well for the position we discussed.

I have a great willingness and eagerness to learn more about EDP auditing, and feel that I am the type of individual who would blend in well with the EDP audit staff at ABC. I look forward to hearing from you.

Sincerely,

Jane Swift
020 8123 4567
jane@anyaddress.co.uk

Follow-up Letter (after face-to-face meeting)
(General Letter)

JANE SWIFT
18 Park Street, London X1 0BB
020 8123 4567   jane@anyaddress.co.uk

[Date]

Phillip _____
[Title]
ABC Ltd
Industry Square
London X2 2EF

Dear Mr _____,

Thank you very much for taking the time to meet me today. I enjoyed our discussion, and I'm now even more excited about the possibility of working for ABC and with your team.

It was great to learn that you are embracing technology as it relates to your business – both in terms of day-to-day operations and the future delivery of ABC's programmes (eg, on-the-spot training). I am very interested in, and have an affinity for, computer technology and would love to be a part of your efforts in this area.

I am confident that I could make a strong contribution to the continued growth of ABC. As we discussed, I have related experience in all of the required areas for the position. In addition, I look forward to taking a project management approach to establishing the new system for the delivery of the assessment workshops to your key client. This process would allow me to ensure that I am meeting your objectives and getting a system 'up and running' within an established time frame. Having done this, I would continually review for improvement and focus on managing the enhancement of customer service.

I remain very interested in the position, and I look forward to hearing from you soon. If you require additional information in the meantime, I may be reached on 020 8123 4567.

Sincerely,

Jane Swift

Jane Swift

Follow-up Letter (after face-to-face meeting)
(Librarian)

JANE SWIFT
18 Park Street, London X1 0BB
020 8123 4567   jane@anyaddress.co.uk

[date]

Mr Philip_____
ABC Library Service
Industry Square
London X2 2EF

Dear Philip,

Thank you for the opportunity to meet you and the selection committee on Monday. I enjoyed our discussion of the Director for Library Development opening. I was impressed with your vision for this individual's role.

Based on our conversation, I believe that I possess the capabilities to successfully meet your expectations for this key position with the Library Service.

To reiterate the experiences I bring to this opportunity, please note the following:

- *Promoting programmes and fostering working relationships with over 1,000 member libraries in all major segments of the field. These activities also encompass extensive community outreach.*
- *Providing strategic vision and mission, and motivating staff to pursue visionary goals. In two leadership assignments, I have recognized staff for their efforts and given them the guidance and direction that has delivered exceptional programme results.*
- *Managing capital projects and spearheading information technology initiatives. These encompassed upgrades to comply with disabled access requirements, renovations that improved space utilization, and leading efforts to incorporate technology into library settings.*
- *Supervising departments in urban and suburban settings to address a broad range of competing priorities. Among these experiences was the supervision of an Interlibrary Loan department serving 100 individual branches in a five-county area.*

I am most interested in this position and am confident that my track record at XYZ demonstrates my capacity to 'hit the ground running', and apply my leadership, enthusiasm, and expertise to furthering the mission of the library service in this development role. I look forward to continuing our discussions in the near future.

Sincerely,

Jane Swift

Jane Swift

Follow-up Letter (after face-to-face meeting)
(Construction Manager)

James Swift
18 Park Street, London X1 0BB
020 8123 4567   james@anyaddress.co.uk

Emily _____   [Date]
[Title]
ABC Ltd
Industry Square
London X2 2EF

Dear Ms _____,

We had the opportunity to speak briefly at last week's Chamber of Commerce meeting concerning the Construction Management position you are seeking to fill in Plymouth. I appreciate you filling me in on the details of the project and have enclosed my CV as you suggested.

As we discussed, I am well acquainted with ABC's brand and store concept, and I am excited to learn of the company's expansion plans over the coming decade. With my background in construction, maintenance and project management as well as operations and strategic leadership, I believe I am primed to play a key role in this growth.

As Chief Executive Officer of XYZ Landscape Design, I have been instrumental in leading the company to phenomenal success within a very short time, building the organization from start-up into a solid revenue generator known throughout the North West as an aggressive competitor in markets crowded by multimillion-pound, nationally recognized companies.

I am currently in the process of selling the company and have been exploring opportunities with dynamic, growth-oriented organizations like yours that could benefit from my broad-based expertise in operations, organizational management, finance and business development. Complementing my diverse leadership background is expertise in all the fundamentals of construction management, including the ability to see projects through to completion while exceeding quality standards.

Perhaps one of my strongest assets is my ability to cultivate long-lasting relationships with clients through attentive, direct communication. I have been highly successful at defining complex project plans, establishing budgets, outlining scope of work, and directly soliciting qualified contractors using the bid process. I also offer extensive experience navigating through the paperwork and bureaucracy, forging productive alliances with key regulatory agencies to streamline permitting and licensing and to facilitate expedited project starts.

I would enjoy the opportunity to speak to you again in greater detail. Could we meet for lunch on Friday? I'll call your assistant in a few days to confirm the appointment.

Best regards,

James Swift

James Swift

Follow-up Letter (after face-to-face meeting)
(Executive Assistant)

JAMES SWIFT
18 Park Street, London X1 0BB
020 8123 4567   james@anyaddress.co.uk

[Date]

Phillip _____
[Title]
ABC Ltd
Industry Square
London X2 2EF

Dear Phillip _____,

The time I spent being interviewed by you and Sandra gave me a clear picture of your company's operation as well as your corporate environment. I want to thank you, in particular, Phillip, for the thorough picture you painted of your CEO's needs and work style.

I left our meeting feeling very enthusiastic about the scope of the position as well as its close match to my abilities and work style. After reviewing your comments, Phillip, I think the key strengths that I can offer your CEO in achieving his agenda are:

- Experience in dealing effectively with senior staff in a manner that facilitates decision-making.
- Proven ability to anticipate an executive's needs and present viable options to consider.
- Excellent communication skills – particularly the ability to gain feedback from staff and summarize succinctly.

Whether the needs at hand involve meeting planning, office administration, scheduling or just serving as a sounding board, I bring a combination of highly effective 'people skills' and diversified business experience to deal with changing situations.

With my energetic work style, I believe that I am an excellent match for this unique position. I would welcome an additional meeting to elaborate on my background and how I can assist your CEO.

Sincerely,

James Swift

James Swift

Follow-up Letter (after face-to-face meeting) (Assistant)

Jane Swift
18 Park Street, London X1 0BB
020 8123 4567   jane@anyaddress.co.uk

[Date]

Emily _____
[Title]
ABC Ltd
Industry Square
London X2 2EF

Dear Ms _____,

Thank you for the opportunity to discuss the position of Assistant.

ABC Ltd is involved in one of the most pressing concerns of today: environmentally safe methods of disposing of solid waste materials. The challenge of creating proper disposal systems is paramount. I look forward to being a part of an organization that is focusing on furthering the technology needed to enhance our environment.

At ABC I would be able to:

- Be a productive assistant to management
- Be a part of a technologically developing industry
- Be in a position to learn and grow with the opportunities presented by your company
- Be involved in the excitement of a new expanding company

The skills that I have to offer ABC Ltd are:

- Professionalism, organization and maturity
- Excellent office skills
- Ability to work independently
- A creative work attitude
- Research and writing skills
- Varied business background
- Willingness to learn

Again, thank you for considering my qualifications to become a part of your organization.

Sincerely,

Jane Swift

Jane Swift

Follow-up Letter (after face-to-face meeting) (Sales)

James Swift
18 Park Street, London X1 0BB
020 8123 4567 james@anyaddress.co.uk

[Date]
Philip_____
[title]
ABC Ltd
Industry Square
London X2 2EF

Philip,

First of all, thank you. I thoroughly enjoyed our meeting last Wednesday, and greatly appreciate your insight and the time taken to discuss where I might best fit in to the ABC team. Your professionalism and willingness to share what you know put me instantly at ease, and I am now even more motivated to be part of ABC's success.

Let me begin by restating how flattered I am that you saw such potential in me. I likewise feel confident that I have the management and leadership expertise, marketing skills and business development experience to be successful, and I see tremendous opportunities for ABC in the future.

However, as we discussed, I understand that my first step is to make my mark as a member of the Road Crew and am equally excited at the opportunity to make an impact on the front line. I realize that you are not currently in a position to make such an offer, but I want to re-emphasize my enthusiasm to join the ABC team wherever you feel I could add value.

If you don't mind, I'd like to take a moment of your time to re-state a few key points:

- I possess the drive, commitment and strong people skills required to make an impact in this industry.
- I offer proven business development, sales and revenue building experience.
- I know what it takes to get results, both out of myself and from others, and have proved again and again to be the 'go to' person when results are expected.

I hope that you and I have the opportunity to continue our discussions and, once again, I appreciate the time you spent with me. I wish you continued success in all your efforts and look forward to seeing you at the *Sales Excellence* seminar at the end of July.

Sincerely,

James Swift

James Swift

Power Phrases

Consider using adaptations of these key phrases in your follow-up letters after face-to-face meetings.

Thank you for meeting me this morning. Our associate _____ assured me that a meeting with you would be productive, and it was. I sincerely appreciate your counsel, insight and advice.

I have attached my CV for your review. I would appreciate any feedback you may have regarding effectiveness and strength. I understand you may not have any searches under way that would be suitable for me at this time, but I would appreciate any future considerations.

Please consider any associates, customers or friends who may have contacts whom it would be useful for me to meet. I have learned how important 'networking' is and would really appreciate some assistance from a professional like you.

Thanks again, _____, and please let me know if I can be of service to you. I wish you and your colleagues continued success and look forward to a business relationship in the future.

In addition to experiencing a very enjoyable and informative interview, I came away very enthusiastic about the position you are seeking to fill.

I hope _____'s consideration of candidates will result in our meeting again soon.

During my drive home I savoured the possibility of working for _____ in the _____ area, and I must say it was an extremely pleasing thought.

I look forward to meeting you again and hope our discussion will precede a long-term working relationship.

I am looking forward to meeting _____ on — August at 10.00 am, at which time I will convince her of my abilities and prove I am the best qualified person for the position.

It was a pleasure meeting you last week in your office. I appreciate the time you spent with me, as well as the valuable information you offered.

I hope you will take a few moments to review my CV and place it in your files for future reference. I will telephone your office next week to discuss my situation further.

Gone but not forgotten ...

Thank you for our time together this afternoon. What I lack in specific experience in your business I more than make up for with my people skills and my proven record of achievement, energy and pure tenacity.

Given the opportunity, I can succeed in your office. That makes you and me both successes. Is that worth the investment in training me?

I would like to take this opportunity to thank you for the interview this morning, and to express my strong interest in the position with _____ .

I would welcome the opportunity to apply and to develop my talents further within your company.

Through my conversations with you and Mr _____ , I felt that the company provides exactly the type of career opportunity that I am seeking, and I am confident that I would prove to be an asset to your organization.

I trust our meeting this morning helped you further define the position. First and foremost, however, I hope that you came away from our meeting with a vision that includes my filling one of the many offices in _____ . I certainly did.

I would like to take this opportunity to thank you for the interview on Thursday morning. I was very impressed with the operation, and I am enthusiastic about the prospect of joining your team.

Since we spent so much time discussing the subject, I have enclosed ...

_I look forward to hearing from you again to further discuss the position. Through my conversations with you and _____, I felt ..._

_After reviewing your comments about the job requirements, I am convinced that I can make an immediate contribution to the growth and profitability of _____._

Since you are going to reach a decision quickly, I would like to mention the following points, which I feel qualify me for the job we discussed: ...

_The position in the _____ area is very attractive to me._

_The interview confirmed that I want this career opportunity. Specifically, I want to work in the _____ department for you and _____. That is the simplest way to say it. I will ring you this week to see what the next step is in the process._

Again, thank you for your time and interest.

It was indeed a pleasure to meet you after working with you by telephone several years ago.

Thank you for taking time out of your busy schedule to meet me on Tuesday, — December, 20—. I left the interview with an extremely favourable impression of your company.

_I would like to take this opportunity to thank you for the interview on Friday morning, and to confirm my strong interest in the _____ position._

_A career opportunity with _____ plc is particularly appealing because of its solid reputation and track record in research and development. I am confident that the training programme and continued sales support will provide me with the background that I need to succeed in a _____ career._

I look forward to discussing my background and the position with you in greater detail.

_I want to take this opportunity to thank you for the interview on Tuesday afternoon, and to confirm my strong interest in the position of _____

with XYZ Healthcare Agency.
From our conversation, I feel confident in my ability to reach and exceed your expectations.

I am looking forward to spending a day in the field with a _____ representative. I will telephone you later this week to set up an appointment for my second interview.

Thank you for your time during my visit to _____ yesterday. I enjoyed our conversation at lunch and learned more about personal trust and investment services.

Thank you for your time and interest today. As I indicated, I am very new to this game of searching for employment and it is nice to start this effort on a positive note.

I am eager to hear from you concerning your decision; I know that you have several other candidates to meet, so I will wait patiently. Good luck to you in your interview process; I know it must be difficult. Again, thank you so much for your time and consideration. I would welcome the opportunity to work for your company.

_____, my visit to your office left me feeling positive about the possibility of working for _____. I would appreciate an opportunity to join your staff, and look forward to hearing from you.

Comments on Follow-up Letter (after face-to-face meeting) (Librarian) (page 200)

The goal of this thank-you letter is two-fold. Obviously, the candidate wants to say 'thank you' for the interview, but she also wishes to reinforce the particular skills and experiences she would bring to the position.

The interview in this case was by a committee and very structured, leaving the candidate feeling that there was more she would have liked to have said. Hence, we used this thank you letter to convey some of these ideas to the committee.

The candidate was employed for this high-level nationwide position.

'Resurrection' E-mail (Account Executive)

Mr _____ ,

I wanted to thank you for the interview on —th March, 20—. The position that was being offered sounds like something I would be interested in. However, I do understand your reasons for not choosing me for the position, and I thank you very much for your honesty.

Perhaps when you are looking for an account executive with five years of experience instead of ten, you will bear me in mind. I am determined to be your choice. I hope the fact that I came in a close second to someone with twice my chronological experience will help you keep me in mind.

I look forward to hearing from you, and thank you again for your time. With your permission I will stay in touch.

Sincerely,

Jane Swift
020 8123 4567
jane@anyaddress.co.uk

'Resurrection' E-mail (Programmer)

Dear Ms _____,

I must have been one of the first people you spoke to about the job, because at the time you seemed very interested in me. However, when I called you back, you had received so many calls for the position, you didn't know one from the other. That's understandable, so I hope I can stir your memory and, more importantly, your interest.

When I spoke to you I got the feeling we could both benefit from working together. I am a computer enthusiast, always looking for new applications and ideas to implement on the computer. I have a solid programming and project development background in both the Windows and Macintosh worlds. What's even better is my hobby: my work. I spend countless hours in one way or another doing things which concern computing.

You had asked if I had children and I do: a four-and-a-half-year-old daughter and a four-and-a-half-month-old daughter. You had some ideas for children's software and thought having kids would help when working on such software. My oldest uses _____ on my Macintosh at home and double-clicks away without any assistance from my wife or myself. She has learned a great deal from 'playing' with it and is already more computer literate than I ever expected. We need more software like _____ to help stir the minds of our kids.

I have attached a CV for your perusal. But in case you don't want to read all the details, here it is in short:

- I have 6 years programming and development experience in Windows.

- I have 3 years programming and development experience on the Macintosh.

- I am currently the Senior Developer for Macintosh programming here at _____ Ltd.

I look forward to speaking to you again, so please don't hesitate to call me, either at home (020 8123 4567) or at work (020 8234 5678) any time.

Regards,

James Swift
020 8123 4567
james@anyaddress.co.uk

'Resurrection' Letter (Wholesale Market Manager)

Jane Swift
18 Park Street, London X1 0BB
020 8123 4567   jane@anyaddress.co.uk

[Date]

Phillip _____
[Title]
ABC Ltd
Industry Square
London X2 2EF

Dear Mr _____,

I understand from _____ of _____ that the search is continuing for the Wholesale Market Manager position at _____ Bank. As you continue your search, I would like to ask that you keep in mind the following accomplishments and experiences that I would bring to the job:

1. Maximized relationships and increased balances through the sale of trust and cash management products.

2. Captured largest share of public funds market in _____ within three years and captured a disproportionate market share of insurance companies in _____.

3. Developed cash management and trust products tailored to the needs of my target market.

4. Marketed services through mass mailings and brochures, through planning and conducting industry-specific seminars, and through active participation in target market's industry professional organization.

5. Direct experience in all phases of wholesale commercial banking, including: market segmentation, prospecting, building and maintaining customer relationships, lending, and the sale of non-credit products and services.

Sincerely,

Jane Swift

Jane Swift

P.S. I will call you next week, after you have seen the other candidates, to continue our discussion. In the meantime, please be assured of both my competency and commitment.

'Resurrection' Letter (Construction Manager)

JAMES SWIFT
18 Park Street, London X1 0BB
020 8123 4567 james@anyaddress.co.uk

[Date]

Alice _____
[Title]
ABC Ltd
Industry Square
London X2 2EF

Dear Ms. _____,

I am writing to you to follow up on the initial enquiry I wrote to you on —th July, 20—. At that time I forwarded you a job search letter and CV. I am in the construction management and business management fields. Since I have not had a response I can only assume that you do not have any vacancies at present that meet my qualifications or that my file has been deactivated.

I am still in the market for an executive position that matches my qualifications and abilities. I am open to relocating throughout the United Kingdom and overseas. If any positions become available, I would be interested in hearing from you. If you need an updated CV, please write or ring me and I would be most happy to forward you any information required.

Sincerely,

James Swift

James Swift

PS. I'll ring in a couple of days to follow up this letter.

Power Phrases

Consider using adaptations of these key phrases in your resurrection letters.

I turned down your job offer, but for reasons I will go into when we meet, I would like to reopen our discussions. If you think such a conversation would be mutually beneficial, I hope we can get together. I'll ring next week to see when you have a half hour or so free.

As you continue your search, I would like to ask that you keep in mind the following accomplishments and experiences that I would bring to the job.

I am still in the market for an executive position that matches my qualifications and abilities. I am open to relocating throughout the United Kingdom and overseas. If any positions become available, I would be interested in hearing from you.

I look forward to hearing from you, and thank you again for your time. With your permission I will stay in touch.

I hope I can stir your memory and, more importantly, your interest.

I look forward to speaking to you again, so please don't hesitate to ring me either at home or at work any time.

Nevertheless, I'm in no position to be proud or disdainful of clerical jobs as I realize I must start somewhere. Fortunately, I enjoy all facets of office work (even filing), so that would not be a problem. I have enough faith in myself and my ability to learn quickly to know that some form of upper movement would be possible for me ... eventually.

Incidentally, even though I am on a temp job this week and possibly next, I do have an answering machine I check every couple of hours during the day. So please leave a message and I'll return your call soon after.

Rejection of Offer E-mail (Department Manager)

Dear Ms _____,

I would like to take this opportunity to thank you for the interview on Thursday morning, and to express my strong interest in future employment with your organization.

While I appreciate very much your offer for the position of Department Manager, I feel that at this stage of my career I am seeking greater challenges and advancement than the Department level is able to provide. Having worked in _____ management for over four years, I am confident that my skills will be best applied in a position with more responsibility and accountability.

As we discussed, I look forward to talking to you again in January about how I might contribute to ABC plc in the capacity of Unit Manager.

Sincere regards,

James Swift
020 8123 4567
james@anyaddress.co.uk

Rejection of Offer Letter (General)

Jane Swift
18 Park Street, London X1 0BB
020 8123 4567   jane@anyaddress.co.uk

[Date]

Phillip _____
[Title]
ABC Ltd
Industry Square
London X2 2EF

Dear Mr _____,

It was indeed a pleasure meeting you and your staff to discuss your needs for a _____.
Our time together was most enjoyable and informative.

As we have discussed during our meetings, I believe a purpose of preliminary interviews is to
explore areas of mutual interest and to assess the fit between the individual and the position.
After careful thought, I have decided to withdraw my application for the position.

My decision is based upon the fact that I have accepted a position elsewhere that is very
suited to my qualifications and experiences.

I want to thank you for interviewing me and giving me the opportunity to learn more about
your facility. You have a fine team, and I would have enjoyed working with you.

Best wishes to you and your staff.

Sincerely,

Jane Swift

Jane Swift

Power Phrases

Consider using adaptations of these key phrases in your rejection of offer letters.

It was indeed a pleasure meeting you and your staff to discuss your needs for a _____.

Our time together was most enjoyable and informative.

After careful thought, I have decided to withdraw my application for the position.

As we discussed, I look forward to talking to you again in _____ about how I might contribute to _____ in the capacity of _____.

Acceptance E-mail (General)

Dear Mr _____,

I would like to express my appreciation for your letter offering me the position of _____ in your _____ Department at a starting salary of £30,000 per year.

I was very impressed with the personnel and facilities at your company in Derby and am writing to confirm my acceptance of your offer. If it is acceptable to you I will report to work on 20 November, 20—.

Let me once again express my appreciation for your offer and my excitement about joining your engineering staff. I look forward to my association with ABC Ltd and feel my contributions will be in line with your goals of growth and continued success for the company.

Sincerely,

James Swift
020 8123 4567
james@anyaddress.co.uk

Acceptance Letter (Marketing Research Manager)

JANE SWIFT
18 Park Street, London X1 0BB
020 8123 4567   jane@anyaddress.co.uk

[Date]

Ms Emily_____
ABC Ltd
Industry Square
London X2 2EF

Dear Ms _____,

Thank you for your positive response to my application for the Marketing Research Manager position. I am delighted to accept your offer of employment and look forward to getting 'stuck in' on the various projects we discussed during our meetings, especially sales forecasting and strategic market planning for ABC's core product line.

I am honoured that your organization feels that I am the right person to lead your marketing research efforts, and am confident that I can deliver the results ABC wants. As I mentioned in our telephone conversation yesterday, I am constantly in touch with what the competition is doing with the goal of placing my team's effort higher in the marketplace to yield maximum results.

As per your instructions, I will contact Mary Smith, Human Resources Manager, on Monday morning to arrange an orientation appointment. I look forward to meeting you after that to discuss in detail my ideas for meeting the objectives we explored in our interviews.

Sincerely,

Jane Swift

Jane Swift

Acceptance Letter (Director)

JAMES SWIFT
18 Park Street, London X1 0BB
020 8123 4567   james@anyaddress.co.uk

[Date]

Emily _____
[Title]
ABC Ltd
Industry Square
London X2 2EF

Dear Ms _____,

This letter will serve as my formal acceptance of your offer to join your firm as Director of _____. I understand and accept the conditions of employment which you explained in your recent letter.

I will contact your personnel department this week to request any paperwork I need to complete for their records prior to my starting date. Also, I will schedule a physical examination for insurance purposes. I would appreciate your forwarding any reading material you feel might hasten my initiation into the affairs of _____.

Yesterday I tendered my resignation at _____ and worked out a mutually acceptable notice time of four weeks, which should allow me ample time to finalize my business and personal affairs here, relocate my family, and be ready for work at _____ on schedule.

You, your board and your staff have been most professional and helpful throughout this process. I eagerly anticipate joining the ABC team and look forward to many new challenges. Thank you for your confidence and support.

Yours truly,

James Swift

James Swift

Negotiation Letter (General)

Jane Swift
18 Park Street, London X1 0BB
020 8123 4567   jane@anyaddress.co.uk

[date]

Mr Philip _____
[Title]
ABC Ltd
Industry Square
London X2 2EF

Dear Philip,

I want to thank you for your invitation to join the ABC family. I have reviewed the offer of position and compensation, as presented in your letter dated _____. I would like to ask for clarification on a few items prior to providing you with a 'formal acceptance'. While none of these items is necessarily a 'deal breaker', I believe they will enable both parties to begin the partnership more informed of mutual goals and expectations.

As per the breakdown provided:

- I accept the bonus scheme as proposed

- I accept the paid holiday and personal days plan as proposed

- I accept the company car plan as proposed

- I accept the Direct Payroll Deposit plan as proposed (if elected)

- I accept the Medical, Dental, Pension and Life Insurance benefits as proposed, contingent on factors clarieid below.

Points of clarification:

- What is available with regards to 'Share Options'?

- What are the 'standard hours of operation' for ABC employees?

- Would it be possible to have a 'Performance Evaluation' at the end of 6 months?

- I would like to structure the holiday entitlement as follows: 3 days in the remainder of the year _____, One week during the calendar year _____, Two weeks during the calendar years _____ – _____, Three weeks beginning January of _____.

- In light of the 'out of pocket expenses' ancipated, how might we agree to get the annual base salary to £35,000? I am open to a number of different options to achieve this goal, including profit sharing, commission, or percentage annual bonus arrangement.

I am excited about the long-term possibilities that exist at ABC. As you can see by my level of interest, I intend to be with you for a long tenure of success. I believe my skills will be an enhancement to the existing leadership. My presence will enable you and others to focus on new aspects of business development and achieve corporate goals and objectives that will be beneficial to us all. Again, I want to thank you for the gracious offer. I look forward to finalizing these minor details very soon.

Sincerely yours,

Jane Swift

Jane Swift

Negotiation Letter (Sales)

James Swift
18 Park Street, London X1 0BB
020 8123 4567   james@anyaddress.co.uk

[Date]

Dear Mr _____,

I have reviewed your letter and the specific breakdown regarding compensation. I believe there to be a few items to clarify, prior to providing you with a formal acceptance. I do not consider any of the items to be 'deal breakers' in any way. I also do not percieve them to be issues that cannot be discussed, as we are in fact moving ahead.

The primary concern has to do with the commission structure, as opposed to salary plus commission, to which I have grown accustomed. I am therefore asking for a one-off initial payment to me of £5000. I am trying to diminish some of the 'exposure' that I may experience in the transition from one office to another. I also believe exposure will be felt as a shift occurs from receipt of compensation on a monthly basis, as I am currently accustomed to a bi-weekly system. Lastly, I am hoping to afford your company the opportunity to share some of the 'risk' in this process and show some 'short-term good faith' towards what I hope will be a long-term relationship of success, productivity and increased profitability.

The second clarification revolves around the bonus scheme: the percentages, time frames and terms. This is something we can discuss over the course of the next weeks. You may even be able to pass on something specific to me in writing.

With these two concerns articulated, I want you to know that I will be meeting the owner of our company tomorrow morning, to discuss my plans for departure. In fairness to him and to my current client load, I could not start full time with you for 21 days.

I would like to set a time for us to have dinner one evening next week, so you can meet my wife and we can talk a little less formally.

Looking forward to what lies ahead,

James Swift

James Swift

Negotation Letter (Senior Lab Specialist)

JAMES SWIFT
18 Park Street, London X1 0BB
020 8123 4567   james@anyaddress.co.uk

[date]

Philip _____
ABC Ltd
Industry Square
London X2 2EF

Dear Philip,

I want to thank you for the time that we were able to spend together last week. I was encouraged by the invitation to join the ABC family as Senior Lab Specialist. The position, responsibility and geography are consistent with my career goals and objectives. Based on the information that you gave to me, there are a number of items that need clarification prior to my providing you with a formal acceptance. None of the items listed is necessarily a 'deal breaker', but they are essential to our beginning this tenure with full disclosure of mutual expectations and responsibilities. Items for clarification are as follows:

- Detailed description of pension benefits
- Realistic analysis of the company shares and bonuses
- Written explanation of the car allowance
- The mobility plan seems very reasonable, but I would like specifics
- Relocation (Is it an allowance or reimbursement of actual expenses incurred in the move?)
- Detailed explanation of the Variable Pay Plan

This final items is significant, as it will have an impact on the 'full compensation potential' and modify the suggested salary. In our conversations, I informed you that I was earning £20k while working part-time and going to college. The salary offer is substantially lower and represents a pay cut. My goal is to discern how feasible it will be for me to meet my financial obligations.

   I am interested in your company and this position, but am finding it difficult to give serious consideration to anything less than a £25k salary plus benefits. I am hoping to discover a variety of means that will enable you to help me achieve that goal, so that I can help you accomplish your growth and profit targets.

   I look forward to discussing these issues with you in the very near future and trust that we will soon be working together in the best interest of Philip _____, James Swift and ABC Ltd.

Respectfully Yours,

James Swift

James Swift

Power Phrases

Consider using adaptations of these key phrases in your acceptance letters.

I am delighted to accept _____'s generous offer to become their _____. All of the terms in your letter of 13th October are acceptable to me.

My resignation was submitted to the appropriate managers at _____ this morning, but we are still working out the terms of my departure.

I am eagerly anticipating starting my new position, particularly at a firm with _____'s reputation. During the interim, I will stay in direct contact with _____ to assure a smooth induction at _____. Thank you again for this opportunity.

We are still working out the terms of my departure from _____, but it is safe to say that I will report to _____ no later than —th November. It should be possible to confirm a starting date early tomorrow morning. I will telephone you directly when my former managers and I have a departure schedule completed.

_____ has scheduled my pre-employment physical for _____, and I do not expect any problems to arise. I have found several possible housing options that I will be investigating and I do not expect any problems here, either.

I appreciate the confidence you demonstrated by selecting me to be _____.

I am confident that you made an excellent choice.

I feel that I can achieve excellent results for your firm, and I am looking forward to working with you. I am also anxious to get to know you and your organization better.

*This letter will serve as my formal acceptance of your offer to join
_____. I understand and accept the conditions of employment that you explained in your recent letter.*

I will contact your personnel department this week to request any paper-work I might complete for their records prior to my starting date. Also, I will schedule a physical examination for insurance purposes. I would appreciate your forwarding any reading material you feel might hasten my initiation into the affairs of _____.

Yesterday I tendered my resignation at _____ and worked out a mutually acceptable notice period of four weeks, which should allow me ample time to finalize my business and personal affairs here, relocate my family, and be ready for work at _____ on schedule.

You, your board, and your staff have been most professional and helpful throughout this process. I eagerly anticipate joining the _____ team and look forward to many new challenges. Thank you for your confidence and support.

I look forward to making a contribution as part of your team.

I look forward to the challenges and responsibility of working in this position.

Resignation E-mail (General)

Dear Mr _____,

This is to notify you that I am resigning my position with ABC Ltd effective Saturday, 26 March, 2000.

I have enjoyed my work here very much and want to thank you and the rest of the MIS Department for all the encouragement and support you have always given me. In order to achieve the career goals that I've set for myself, I am accepting a higher level Systems Operator position with another company. This position will give me an opportunity to become more involved in the technical aspects of setting up networking systems.

I am more than happy to help with any staff training or offer assistance in any way that will make my departure as easy as possible for the department. I want to wish everyone the best of luck for the future.

Sincerely,

James Swift
020 8123 4567
james@anyaddress.co.uk

Resignation Letter (Sales Representative)

JAMES SWIFT
18 Park Street, London X1 0BB
020 8123 4567   james@anyaddress.co.uk

[Date]

Phillip _____
[Title]
ABC Ltd
Industry Square
London X2 2EF

Dear Mr _____,

Please accept my resignation from my position as Sales Representative in the _____ area, effective — January, 20—. I am offering two weeks' notice so that my territory can be serviced effectively during the transition, with the least amount of inconvenience to our clients.

While I have very much enjoyed working under your direction, I find now that I have an opportunity to develop my career further in areas that are more in line with my long-term goals. I thank you for the sales training that I have received under your supervision. It is largely due to the excellent experience I gained working for ABC Ltd that I am now able to pursue this growth opportunity.

During the next two weeks, I am willing to help you in any way to make the transition as smooth as possible. This includes assisting in recruiting and training my replacement in the _____ region. Please let me know if there is anything specific that you would like me to do.

Again, it has been a pleasure working as a part of your group.

Best regards,

James Swift

James Swift

Resignation Letter (Director)

JANE SWIFT
18 Park Street, London X1 0BB
020 8123 4567   jane@anyaddress.co.uk

[Date]

Emily _____
[Title]
ABC Ltd
Industry Square
London X2 2EF

Dear Ms _____,

As of this date, I am formally tendering my resignation as _____. I have accepted a position as Director of _____ at a university medical centre in _____.

My decision to leave ABC Ltd was made after long and careful consideration of all factors affecting the company, my family and my career. Although I regret leaving many friends here, I feel that the change will be beneficial to all parties. My subordinate is readily able to handle the company's operations until you find a suitable replacement. I intend to finalize my business and personal affairs here over the next few weeks and will discuss a mutually acceptable termination date with you in person.

Finally, I can only express my sincere appreciation to you and the entire board for all your support, cooperation and encouragement over the years. I will always remember my stay at ABC for the personal growth it afforded and for the numerous friendships made.

Yours truly,

Jane Swift

Jane Swift

Power Phrases

Consider using adaptations of these key phrases in your resignation letters.

I am offering two weeks' notice so that my territory can be serviced effectively during the transition, with the least amount of inconvenience to our clients.

While I have very much enjoyed working under your direction, I now find that I have an opportunity to develop my career further in areas that are more in line with my long-term goals. I thank you for the sales training that I have received under your supervision. It is largely due to the excellent experience I gained working for ABC that I am now able to pursue this growth opportunity.

During the next two weeks, I am willing to help you in any way to make the transition as smooth as possible. This includes assisting in recruiting and training my replacement in the _____ region. Please let me know if there is anything specific that you would like me to do.

Again, it has been a pleasure working as a part of your sales force.

I have thoroughly enjoyed the work environment and professional atmosphere at _____. Your guidance and counselling have been the source of great personal and career satisfaction, and I am grateful.

These _____ years have made a considerable contribution to my career and professional development and I hope that I have likewise contributed during this time to the growth and development of ABC Ltd. I am grateful for the kind of associates I have had the opportunity to work with and the substantial support I have consistently received from management.

Thank-you E-mail (after appointment)
(Software Manager)

Dear Ms _____,

I am happy to inform you that I received and accepted an offer of employment just after Christmas. I am now employed by _____.

I would also like to thank you for all your help in recent months not only in my search for employment but also by your understanding and friendly words of encouragement.

My duties include responsibility for all accounting software (General Ledger, Accounts Payable, Accounts Receivable, and Fixed Assets) for _____ worldwide plus the first-year training of several entry-level employees.

I am enjoying my new responsibility and being fully employed again, although at times I feel overwhelmed with all I have to learn.

If there is ever anything I can do for you please ring me. I hope you and your family have a wonderful Christmas and wish you much luck and happiness in the new year.

Sincerely,

James Swift
020 8123 4567
james@anyaddress.co.uk

Thank-you Letter (after appointment) (General)

JAMES SWIFT
18 Park Street, London X1 0BB
020 8123 4567   james@anyaddress.co.uk

[Date]

Phillip _____
[Title]
ABC Ltd
Industry Square
London X2 2EF

Dear Mr _____,

I want you to be among the first to know that my job search has come to a very successful conclusion. I have accepted the position of _____ at _____, located in _____.

I appreciate all the help and support you have provided over the last few months. It has made the job search process much easier for me. I look forward to staying in contact with you. Please let me know if I can be of any assistance to you in the future. Thank you.

Sincerely,

James Swift

James Swift

Power Phrases

Consider using adaptations of these key phrases in your thank you letters.

I am writing to share this good news with you and to thank you for your efforts on my behalf. If there is ever anything that I can do for you, please do not hesitate to ring me.

Thank you for all your help. I have accepted a position as a _____ for _____.

I want you to be among the first to know that my job search has come to a very successful conclusion.

I appreciate all the help and support you have provided over the last few months. It has made the job search process much easier for me. I look forward to staying in contact with you. Please let me know if I can be of any assistance to you in the future.

I would like to extend my sincere thanks to you for your kind help and encouragement during my job search. If I can be of any assistance to you in the future, please do not hesitate to contact me. I was often reminded during the past few months that we too easily lose contact with old friends. Let's try to stay in touch.

If you ever get a chance to visit _____, on business or pleasure, please be sure to let me know.

If there is ever anything I can do for you, please ring me. I hope you and your family have a wonderful Christmas and wish you much luck and happiness in the new year.

Just a quick note to bring you up to date with what I am doing.

Appendix: How to Jump-Start a Stalled Job Search

A short course on getting your job search back on track.

Jerry has been out of work now for a year. His redundancy package was really lousy – a week for every year of service, which amounted to seven weeks for him. The house, two cars and three kids should have provided enough pressure to get Jerry's backside in gear, but they didn't.

Jerry told me that no one was phoning him. No one would return his calls. It was a bad time of year, he would say, or his contacts were all stale. Often, he would just express amazement and bewilderment as to how he could be in such a predicament.

There was no mystery here. He wasn't getting calls because he wasn't making calls in the right way. When he did dial a headhunter or a personnel department, his tone was so negative that he rarely got through the first screen. He was mailing out CVs, but just a handful each week, and he didn't even follow up on these. Jerry was scared and frightened of the search process, and the financial pressures made him so anxious that he wasn't able to do what he needed to do to land a job. Jerry became terrified by what he saw as his failure.

For Bob, the story is different. He has a job. It's not yet 9 o'clock, but Bob is already complaining about what a lousy place this is to work. His boss is a moron – can you believe what he did last week? The pay is low, the benefits poor, and the cafeteria serves inedible rubbish. He winds up with 'I've got to get out of here'. You'd guess that good old Bob is mounting a huge job search campaign, and that he's got one foot out the door. You'd guess wrong. Bob's not going anywhere, at least not under his own steam.

He is frightened of making an effort, taking the plunge, and then finding that he can't make the grade. So, instead, he hides out in a dead-end job, with a going-nowhere company, letting his fears conquer the soul of his work life. Bob and Jerry have both allowed their fear to stall their job search.

For Bob and Jerry, or for you, if your job search is stalled, there is hope – if you are prepared to take very small but very important steps to change your work-life situation. Write down all of your thoughts about yourself, your career and your job situation. All of them. Just put everything down on paper; don't edit anything. Then read them aloud. First to yourself, and then to a trusted friend or colleague. Ask for feedback. Ask the other person to tell you whether they agree or disagree with what you've written. Start to understand your negative thoughts and begin to discover who you *really* are.

When Failure Feels Like Forever

Fear of failure is so hateful to us, so threatening, that we'll do whatever we possibly can to avoid it. As bad as your job situation is right now, your fear of failure is even worse. So you stall, you procrastinate and you point the finger of blame, but you don't see the other three fingers pointing right back at you.

You can tell me that you are actually doing everything you can to get a job – everything you can imagine. You can be working like the devil on a search, but doing all of the wrong things. You might tell yourself and the world that, yes, you are trying to get a job. But in your heart of hearts, you may have doubts about the way you are going about it. Don't feel distraught; lots of people feel the same way. Job hunting and career management are not skills you were taught in school or anywhere else.

Evaluate your search. Are you being realistic? Are you working intelligently at your job search? Are you really doing all of the right things, or are you rationalizing doing what is comfortable? Or are you avoiding failure by making dumb decisions and then hiding behind them?

If your job search seems hopeless, try to understand what you get out of *not* doing what it takes to get a good job. How do you feel when that rejection letter comes? Do friends or relatives pester you by asking how the search is going, or whether you got the job? If you have to tell them that no, you didn't get the job, do you feel like a failure?

However, if you are stalling about getting your search in gear, think about what that will get you. What are you getting out of not looking for a job? Are you avoiding the rejection that is a big part of every job search? Are you escaping from the many *nos* you will have to hear before you hear *yes* from the lips of an employer?

If you are engaged in a genuine job hunt, I can guarantee that you will fail along the way. I hope that you will fail many, many times. If you don't, then you're not looking hard enough. Every job search involves failure and rejection. If you are networking, making phone calls, doing your research, sending out CVs, going to interviews with prospective employers and responding to ads, then you are creating hundreds of chances for rejection, hundreds of opportunities to hear the word *no*. This rejection must happen if you want to get out of your present situation! I can't tell you that it's a lot of fun to get rejection letters, or to have people hang up on you. It's never an enjoyable thing. It is a fact of life, and you can develop the ability you need to overcome rejection.

Lock and Load

OK. You've been out of work for a while. You're low on ideas, and your petrol tank reads 'empty'. You don't know which way to turn. The things you've done so far just haven't worked out. It's time to take it from the top.

Believe it or not, you can start over again, and you have certain advantages in doing so. At least some of the people who screened you out so many months ago have, in all likelihood, moved on to another place. Sure, most of the jobs you applied for have been filled, but a whole new batch has now opened up. And, if there were ill economic winds blowing through an industry you took a fancy to, perhaps things are now looking up for some of the companies on your list.

With a few adjustments here and there, and a bit more attention to a few points, you can rescue a faltering job search and get yourself back to work.

Getting Unstuck

If you are stuck, if your search is not working well, it's time to try things that may have seemed unnecessary or gimmicky earlier in your search. It's time to get unstuck – by any means necessary:

■ Send copies of your job search activity list, including names of companies to phone, numbers of CVs to be sent out each week, etc, to two or three colleagues or friends. Have them ring you on key dates to check up on you. Don't say you don't need supervision, and don't worry if it's embarrassing. Chances are, you do need help, and chances are, your friends would love to have a concrete way to help you. This is the time to put peer pressure and shame to work for you. If your friends can't help you, join a local job-hunting group; your peers can help you, and you can help your peers.

■ Reward yourself for progress in your search. Keep an account of your activities. When you reach a target (say 25 CVs sent out this week, and 25 follow-up calls made on the 25 CVs you sent out last week), then you can cash them in for a fun activity. At this point, that fun activity may be a morning of not having to do something you hate to do, like making follow-up calls on CVs.

■ Don't get overwhelmed by irrelevant details. Create a personal 'parking space' for non-essential activities. A good meeting facilitator puts up a piece of paper in the front of the meeting room. When someone makes a comment that is off the topic, the facilitator writes it down on that paper. If there's time, or if the topic comes up again, the idea is pulled out of the 'parking space' for discussion. The meeting stays focused, and the person with the idea hasn't forgotten about it. Don't throw out your non-essential ideas. Park them instead. When you have time, after you achieve your most essential objectives, visit the 'parking space' and take an old idea out for a spin.

■ Break up major tasks into small steps. Don't write 'find a job' on your to-do list. Instead, make a list of the many steps you need to find a job, using this book. As you complete each step, tick it off. Save the ticked-off list so that you can see yourself making progress.

Sometimes, being a procrastinator is due to not knowing any better. There are many books and courses on priority management. They can help you give some order to your to-do list, and help you avoid the feeling of being overwhelmed. Managing priorities is a very learnable behaviour!

Get a New CV

White collar or blue collar, executive director or electrician, you should throw out whatever you've got and start again from scratch, because the current version obviously isn't working. Write at least two new drafts. One should be in chronological format; the other should be in either functional or combination format.

Don't pooh-pooh the idea of rewriting your CV by claiming that getting your foot in the door hasn't been the problem. It is entirely possible that your CV is strong enough to get you in the race, but doesn't pack enough punch to push you over the finishing line. Your CV must get your foot in the door, set the tone for the interview and, after all the interviewing is done, act as your last and most powerful advocate when the final decision is being made. Build one from ground up that does this.

Rewrite Your Job Search Letter

Adhering to a single, bland, 'one-size-fits-all' job search letter is a common mistake. Remember, different circumstances require different letters.

I would advise you to make a commitment to send follow-up letters with religious zeal, if you are not already doing so. This may seem like a minor detail, but it is one of the most important – and easiest – ways for you to stand out from the competition.

When it comes to job search and follow-up letters, the whole really is greater than the sum of its parts. Employers maintain dossiers on every candidate during the selection process; your coordinated written campaign makes you stand out from the other contenders as someone who pays a little bit more attention to detail and who goes a little further to get the job done. Don't worry about sending your new CV to companies you've already contacted. A new CV means a new you.

Work As a Temporary

Get hold of a temporary employment directory or check the *Yellow Pages* for temporary agencies. Contact every appropriate agency listed for your area and offer your services.

There are two benefits to working with a temporary agency. First, while you can retain time to pursue a structured job hunt, you also get some work and get paid – thereby keeping your skills current and, just as important, the wolf from the door. Second, you may be able to upgrade that temporary job into a full-time position. (At the very least, you can expand your contact network.)

Today, there are temporary agencies that represent professionals at virtually all levels. Some even specialize solely in management people, and high-level ones at that, because companies are increasingly inclined to 'test-drive' executives before making a permanent commitment to them.

Check Your References

Do it now. You'd be surprised how many otherwise qualified candidates eventually learn that they were taken out of the running by failing the 'tie-breaker' test. Two or more people are under final consideration; management decides to call your referees to help them decide who will get the job. If you have not attended to tthis area, you should: mediocre (or worse) references can undo months of preparation on your part.

Widen the Scope of Your Job Search

Under what other job titles could you work? Can you commute an extra 20 minutes for the right job? Consider relocation to another city, but bear in mind that, for most of us, this is an extremely costly proposition and that you should not depend on a firm's picking up your moving expenses. On the other hand, if you are single and can fit all your earthly possessions in the back seat of your car, some far-flung operation may be worth serious consideration.

Incorporate job hunting as part of your daily routine. Stop in and see what firms are in that office building you pass every morning. Perhaps there are opportunities there for you.

Of course, you are not going to get far by simply appearing at the reception desk and demanding an interview. Be a little more circumspect. Ask – politely – about the firm in question. What does it do? Who is in charge of recruitment? Are there any circulars, advertisements or company reports you can take home with you? After your initial visit, you can incorporate this information into a new research file for the company and add the firm to your database of leads.

This, by the way, is the job hunting technique I personally loathe more than any other; but it was also the technique that landed the job that – 22 years later – has obviously given me a buoyant career. The fact that you don't like a particular job hunting technique doesn't mean it won't work for you.

Body Check

If you find yourself running into brick walls on the job search front, it's a good idea to look at the most important points more thoroughly. Remember, your personal friends often have trouble bringing up this subject; people in a position to employ simply move on to the next applicant.

If you do not brush and floss regularly, and have bad breath, this will not aid your candidacy. If you eat a lot of spicy foods (onions, garlic), you may be aware of the importance of keeping your breath fresh after a pungent meal but this is not, alas, your only worry. These foods typically sour your sweat and taint your clothing. Change your diet and have your interview clothes cleaned before every wearing. (But note that polyester and other synthetic fabrics are notorious for retaining body odours even after cleaning – one of many reasons to avoid them.)

Have you put on a few pounds while looking for work? Many people use eating as a response to stress. Turn off the TV once a day and get some exercise. Couch potatoes don't make good candidates. Regular physical activity will improve your appearance *and* your mindset, so don't skip it.

These suggestions may be difficult for you to implement if they run counter to long-established patterns, but being in a permanent job search mode is, you must admit, a much more daunting prospect than change. If you need motivation, recall the statistical truth that overweight and malodorous people are always the last to be employed or promoted.

Prepare, Prepare, Prepare

It may seem obvious, but all too often this is the step that people take for granted. When you walk into the interview, you should be ready to answer all the questions you could ever be asked, as well as all the ones you couldn't. *Don't* make the mistake of preparing only for the questions you want to hear!

Follow Up

I worked for some years as a headhunter and corporate personnel director. I can't count the number of times managers told me that there was really nothing to distinguish Candidate A (who got the job) from Candidate B (who didn't) – *except that Candidate A showed an unusual level of determination and attention to detail.* The way Candidate A conveyed this, of course, was usually through a dogged follow-up campaign.

Stepping Stone Jobs

Even though this has been touched on earlier in this book, it bears repeating in this context. If you have been unemployed for a significant period of time, you might find it fiscally prudent to accept that less-than-perfect job. That's OK. By the same token, there is a big difference between settling for less than your dreams and making the wrong job your life's work. If circumstances force you to take a temporary detour from your ultimate career goal, give an honest day's work for an honest day's pay, and continue to pursue other opportunities.

Remember: You're the Most Important Part of This

Maintain ongoing motivational input. Reading this book and its companion book, *The Ultimate CV Book* is a good start. You should also consider going online or visiting the library to check out motivational tapes and related materials. You're worth it.

You are not a loser; you got knocked off course. The trick is to get back in the saddle. If you climb up and grip the reins, tomorrow you'll see all kinds of opportunities you didn't see before. You can get back on track, and you can get back to work.

Index